Anatomy and Disease

Medical Transcription Program
3rd Edition

Career Step, LLC
Phone: 801.489.9393
Toll-Free: 800.246.7837
Fax: 801.491.6645
careerstep.com

This text companion contains a snapshot of the online program content converted to a printed format. Please note that the online training program is constantly changing and improving and is always the source of the most up-to-date information.

Table of Contents

Unit 1
Introduction

Human Anatomy and Disease Processes – Introduction

Learning Objective

The purpose of this module is to introduce the student to basic human anatomical structures and the various diseases that affect them. The student will be introduced to disease entities, diagnoses, and treatments.

Human anatomy and disease processes are an integral part of medical terminology. Understanding the body, its mechanisms, parts, and disease processes will prove tremendously helpful during transcription. In fact, some of the most commonly used medical words and phrases deal with basic human anatomy or body structures.

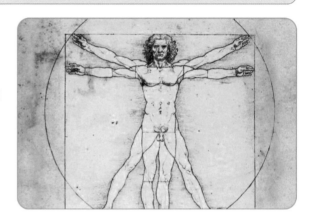

However, medical transcription as a career deals largely with practical-application medical terms. This means that you as a transcriptionist are not likely to be transcribing research summaries, theories, or theoretical papers (although occasionally a paragraph or two may be required in a medical report or correspondence).

Therefore, it is highly unlikely that you will get into any detailed or theoretic postulations on medical principles. Instead, you will be deciphering the physical manifestations a patient has been experiencing, his/her actual presentation (this includes the examination, as well as any laboratory tests, x-rays, or other types of studies), the treatment of any problems, reactions to treatment rendered, and any future suggestions for the patient.

The objective of this module is to give you a basic understanding of anatomy and disease. Do not be overwhelmed by everything in this module. You are not expected to be a doctor or to know everything that a doctor knows. It is neither your responsibility nor your right to change, in a fundamental way, anything a dictator diagnoses, treats, or prescribes. In fact, doing so will probably get you fired. It is the case, however, that you may be able to easily locate a word or understand a sentence in a report because you know the meaning of a word or the location in the body to which a specific term refers.

It is imperative you have at least a rudimentary understanding of bones, muscles, arteries, veins, ligaments, joints, and organs to be an effective MT. The more terms you are familiar with, the less time you will spend wandering aimlessly through your reference books.

As you begin, you will be spending a great deal of time trying to decipher what a dictator might be saying and then looking for the correct spelling of that word (or combinations of words) in a dictionary or online resource. Of course, it is not feasible for you to look up everything you don't completely understand. It is up to you, the student, how much energy and mental power you will choose to devote to this aspect of your training. By investing more time now, you will undoubtedly spend less time searching through your reference books later. In any case, if you have seen and transcribed a word in the past, it would be easier to recall.

Having an understanding of basic anatomy and where parts are located, and coupling that with an understanding of disease processes, will significantly increase your speed and accuracy in completing a medical report. You will also become a valuable asset as an employee in a job setting, for you will not inadvertently use an inappropriate word because you are unsure of its meaning and/or if it will fit in the sentence.

Again, it is not totally essential to know, as a doctor would be required to know, every minute detail of the human anatomy. It is unnecessary to learn and be able to correctly label every system and structure of the body. Doing so would be prohibitively time consuming, and it is overkill.

You should, however, be able to spell medical terms correctly and know approximately where they are located in the body. (For example, you should be able to recognize whether a specific term refers to a bone or vein). Furthermore, understanding of the diseases, or what could go wrong with the body, is especially helpful because it is exactly what you will be typing as a transcriptionist. It will make your research easier as well. All of this should come together to help you identify what a doctor is saying based on the context of the report, and you will avoid wasting your valuable time looking up all possible spellings and reading corresponding definitions to guarantee accuracy—because, of course, accuracy is extremely important.

This module contains several figures representing different anatomical parts of the human body, labeled appropriately, as well as textual information regarding the anatomical parts. You should be familiar with all labeled body structures. You will be given the opportunity, often, to not only see a term written, but to experience transcribing it yourself. Entering the terms in the spaces provided will reinforce the spelling in your mind and make you faster. It will also get you accustomed to seeing the word transcribed and spelled correctly. Being able to pick a misspelled word out of a report is a valuable skill.

Again, for the purposes of this module and the terminology lists, spelling should be your primary concern as a transcriptionist. Notice first what type of word it is (for example, a muscle or an artery) and where in the body it is located (for example, extremities, torso, or head). While a majority of your exercises in this module are centered around the spelling of medical words, you will also be required to answer questions relating to word differentiation and disease processes.

In the units that follow, you should notice similarities between the names of arteries, veins, bones, ligaments, nerves, and muscles and where they are found in the body. Specifically, you may see the same word appear in reference to many of these structures. For example, a bone of the forearm is called the ulna. There is, consequently, an ulnar nerve, ulnar artery, ulnar ligament, radioulnar joint, etc. The exercises in this module will give you experience identifying the appropriate spelling and writing the same words in several different situations. Notice also that when the same term is used multiple times for different structures, they are in the same area of the body, as noted in the example of ulna/ulnar. This makes your job of knowing the spelling and approximate body location much easier.

This module provides supplemental information on different physiological and anatomical structures and body systems. However, the information is fairly basic, on a par with high school or freshman-level college anatomy. Use the information to reiterate the portions of anatomy and disease that are relevant to medical transcription. You will also be given tips about when and where you are likely to see the terms you are learning in a real world environment.

It could be said that medicine itself is simply the diagnosis and treatment of disease. It is impossible to overestimate the importance of understanding something about disease processes and relating it to the medical reports you will eventually be transcribing. All of these terms will become a part of your daily life as a transcriptionist.

In the following units, you will also learn what types of injuries and diseases relate to a particular part of the human body. Although there are far too many individual diseases, syndromes, injuries, signs, and treatments for you to learn every one of them here, we have made every effort to include the most common ones. It may or may not be the case that your job as an MT will require a broad knowledge of all types of medical reports, as we cover in this module, but your marketability will increase with every term you learn and can identify either by spelling or by meaning.

Tip for Success in Anatomy and Disease

As you work through this module, try not to be overwhelmed by all of the information. You are not expected to know everything, and you will have ample opportunity to look things up to determine meaning or verify appropriate context. Concentrate on developing and fine tuning your editing skills. Does a word or a sentence look correct to you? Why or why not? Pay close attention to portions of this module that relate what you are learning to what you will eventually be doing. This is what you will actually be transcribing, both in the training program and in the real world.

Unit 2
Disease Processes

Disease Processes – Introduction

In order to gain an understanding of specific pathologies, it is necessary first to know what is meant by the term *disease*, as well as know some general terms by which diseases are classified. There are consistencies in terminology which you will see throughout the body and its systems and, consequently, in all types of medical reports.

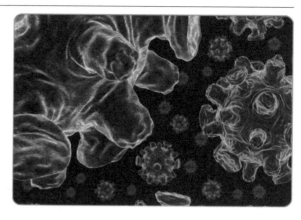

Disease: Any deviation from or interruption of the normal structure or function of any part, organ or system (or any combination thereof) of the body that is manifested by a characteristic set of symptoms and signs, and whose etiology, pathology, and prognosis may be known or unknown.*

The term *disease* is a fairly generic term meaning a condition of abnormal functioning. In any case, with such a broad definition, it is correct to say that modern medicine, for all intents and purposes, is simply the identification and treatment of disease processes. This is true regardless of the type of specialty or nature of the disease. A family physician may spend more time examining injuries, listening to breathing, and testing for strep throat than prescribing antibiotics or administering stitches. By the same token, a cardiothoracic surgeon tries to identify what is causing abnormal heart symptoms, clears plaque out, and repairs arteries in lengthy and difficult surgery. Regardless of the specialty or the problem, it all comes down to identifying problems with the human body and fixing them.

Consider the diagnostic process step by step using theoretical patient A. Patient A identifies something as being wrong with his body. He experiences a symptom or set of symptoms. This can be any distress, dysfunction, or abnormality whatsoever. A combination of symptoms that occur together is called a syndrome. Many specific kinds of syndromes can be found in a medical dictionary or word book listed under *syndrome*. In any case, if patient A, who is experiencing one or more symptoms, wants to be symptom-free and feel better, he will often go to a medical practitioner. As a medical transcriptionist, you will be transcribing reports detailing what happens from that point on.

The doctor, nurse, or physician's assistant will initially need to ascertain what patient A's symptoms are and secondly what is causing them. There is, of course, a word for this causative factor. The term *etiology* refers to the cause or origin of a disease or disorder. Basically, when a patient has symptoms, the practitioner looks for the etiology or cause of those symptoms. There are several different methods of determining what the disease process in a human being is. You will become familiar with these methods as you begin transcribing because they are an integral part of every report you will transcribe.

The first step in determining the reason for a patient's symptoms is to obtain a history. This is sometimes called the subjective, since the patient reports his or her own feelings and symptoms. It is obviously a very important part of the diagnostic process. For example, if your arm hurts, it may help the doctor to know that you crushed it under a tractor.

Secondly, it will be necessary for the doctor to perform an objective examination. A part of this is called a physical examination. Most (probably even all) of you have probably undergone such an exam. Depending upon the severity of your symptoms, you will have all or only a portion of your body and systems examined. There are some specific procedures which are commonly performed in physical examinations that you will need to learn. Auscultation is listening to selected organs (usually the heart and lungs) with a stethoscope. Inspection is just what it sounds like—looking at the parts of the body that are affected (mouth, nose, ears, skin, etc.). Palpation means the act of feeling with the hands and fingers. It is feeling through the skin for masses, tenderness, spasms, swelling, or other abnormalities. Percussion is tapping with a finger on the body wall to try to detect variations in the sound over masses, fluid, or air pockets. Physical examinations also check reflexes and *signs*. These are activities that a doctor has a patient perform or physical evidences that a doctor is aware of that a patient may not be aware of. There are many different types of signs.

The physical examination can be a very brief description of the affected area (examination of the knees, for example), or a long, detailed paragraph describing every system of the body. We cover physical exams thoroughly in the Building the Medical Record module. You will see oodles of examples of physical examinations in the Focus on Medical Specialties module as well. It is mentioned here to help you better understand how diseases are diagnosed.

Another objective method of determining the etiology of a patient's symptoms is to perform diagnostic tests. These range from drawing blood and testing blood chemistries to performing operations. The reason for performing tests in a medical setting is to find out exactly what the disease or problem is. In the event of a possible fracture, for example, an x-ray can give the doctor a clear picture of the potentially affected bones and reveal any cracks, soft tissue swelling, or broken fragments. By the same token, an operation like a biopsy can remove an obviously abnormal piece of bone or tissue and send it to a pathologist, who then performs general and microscopic examinations to determine the nature and causation of the abnormality.

In addition to radiological and pathological examinations, there are a variety of laboratory tests that can aid in diagnosing medical problems. Some examples of laboratory tests are CTs and MRIs, endoscopy procedures, microbiology, serology (which tests reactions to antigens), and full scale operations.

(Dorland's Medical Dictionary, 31st Ed., 2007)

Descriptive Terms – Lesson 1

Medical practitioners use descriptive disease-related terminology both when working with patients and when dictating a variety of reports, including the history and physical examination, diagnostic testing, clinic notes, and operative procedures, to name a few. There are many descriptive terms that are used to classify diseases. Following is a list of terms that describe where the disease comes from or what causes it. In an effort to better acquaint yourself with the terms and their proper spelling, complete the following exercises.

  I. TERMINOLOGY.
      Enter each term in the space provided. Read the definition and description for each term.

  1. **deficiency** _____

  A lack or defect. Many diseases are caused by a lack of some vital chemical substance or compound, such as red blood cells (anemia) or oxygen (hypoxia).

  2. **degenerative** _____

  Pertaining to deterioration. Going from a normal form to a lower or more dysfunctional form. The deterioration of certain structures or tissues leads to many different diseases, such as degenerative joint disease or Alzheimer disease.

  3. **developmental** _____

  Occurs as a result of some abnormality in the development of tissue, an organ, or body part. These are usually characterized as disorders which occur before birth or during the growth stages, such as osteodystrophy.

  4. **essential** _____

  Term assigned to diseases for which the cause is unknown. It is assumed that it arises spontaneously, such as essential hypertension.

5. **familial** _____

Occurring in or affecting more members of a family than would be expected by chance, such as familial hypertrophic cardiomyopathy.

6. **functional** _____

Due to a disturbance of function without evidence of a structural or chemical abnormality. An example is menorrhea or menorrhagia that cannot be explained by fibroids, endometriosis, infection, or some other obvious cause.

7. **hereditary** _____

Means genetically transmitted from parent to offspring. This term should be familiar. As with any trait—eye color, hair color, height, etc.—diseases can be genetically transferred. Examples include hemophilia, dyslexia, and asthma.

II. **SPELLING.**
Determine if the following words are spelled correctly. If the spelling is correct, leave the word as it has already been entered. If the spelling is incorrect, provide the correct spelling.

1. deficeincy _____
2. degeneraitive _____
3. developmentil _____
4. essential _____
5. familail _____
6. funcktional _____
7. hereditery _____

Descriptive Terms – Lesson 2

I. **TERMINOLOGY.**
Enter each term in the space provided. Read the definition and description for each term.

1. **idiopathic** _____

Of unknown cause, arising spontaneously, such as idiopathic cardiomyopathy.

2. **infectious** _____

Caused by an infection. (Doesn't that state the obvious?) An infection is the invasion and multiplication of microorganisms in body tissue. There are many different types of bacteria that cause infection and infective diseases, such as pneumonia and mononucleosis. Other infectious agents are viruses and fungi.

3. **molecular** _____

Caused by abnormality in the chemical structure or concentration of a single molecule (the smallest amount of a substance which can exist alone), usually a protein or enzyme. Molecular diseases are often also congenital, such as sickle cell anemia.

4. **neoplastic** _____

Pertaining to any new and abnormal growth, specifically a new growth of tissue which is progressive and uncontrolled. These growths are generally called tumors. A neoplasm can be either benign or malignant. Malignant means tending to become progressively worse, resulting in death. Benign is simply the opposite of malignant. Cancer is a neoplastic disease.

5. **nutritional** _____

Causation is due to nutritional factors, either insufficient or excessive dietary intake. Common nutritional diseases are eating disorders, such as bulimia or anorexia nervosa. Scurvy and rickets are examples of diseases caused by poor nutrition and/or vitamin deficiency.

6. **organic** _____

Due to a demonstrable abnormality in a bodily structure, such as a heart murmur.

7. **traumatic** _____

Resulting from some type of injury: physical, chemical, or psychological. Many pathologies fall into this category, such as fractures, burns, dislocations, cuts, injuries from motor vehicle or other accidents, war wounds, or the psychological effects of abuse, war or rape, leading to diseases such as post-traumatic stress disorder.

II. **SPELLING.**
   Determine if the following words are spelled correctly. If the spelling is correct, leave the word as it has already been entered. If the spelling is incorrect, provide the correct spelling.

   1. ideopathic _____   2. infectous _____

   3. mollecular _____   4. neoplastic _____

   5. nutritoinal _____   6. oarganic _____

   7. traumatic _____

Symptomatic Terms – Lesson 1

Symptoms are also (as you might imagine) helpful in diagnosing, treating, and classifying diseases. When a medical professional has communication with a patient, often times terminology dealing with symptoms is used. Information such as onset of symptoms, duration of time experienced, severity, and when symptoms disappeared are all important pieces of information used in diagnosing, treating, and classifying diseases. The following is a list of terms that deal with disease symptoms. In an effort to better acquaint yourself with the terms and their proper spelling, complete the following exercises.

I. TERMINOLOGY.

Enter each term in the space provided. Read the definition and description for each term.

1. acquired _____

Patient was not born with it (it was not hereditary or congenital). Recently the most talked about disease of this type is AIDS—which stands for acquired immunodeficiency syndrome.

2. acute _____

One which has a short and relatively severe course. A patient with an acute illness has not been experiencing symptoms for very long. Acute appendicitis, for example, is common. This is inflammation of the appendix which develops quickly and often necessitates surgery because of the likelihood of the appendix bursting. (Of note, this does not refer to how a disease looks—a cute little disease.)

3. asymptomatic _____

Having no symptoms. Although generally individuals do not go to a doctor or hospital when they are not experiencing symptoms, underlying asymptomatic diseases are often discovered during examinations which are either routine or being performed for a different reason.

4. chronic _____

Persisting over a long period of time. This is the opposite of an acute illness. A chronic condition can last for years and sometimes a lifetime. An example is chronic bronchitis, which results in daily or constant coughing and changes in the lung tissue.

5. congenital _____

Present at birth. This differs from a hereditary condition in that it is not necessarily inherited from the parents. Occasionally infants are born with congenital heart defects which can require surgery or lead to death.

6. disabling _____

Causes impairment of normal functions, such as sight, hearing, mobility, or breathing.

7. end-stage _____

A progressively deteriorating condition, such as end-stage liver disease, that has reached a point of terminal functional impairment of the affected organ or system.

8. intermittent _____

Causes symptoms at intervals with periods of time between them with no symptoms. Most coughs, for example, are intermittent.

II. MATCHING.
   Match the appropriate terms below. Enter only the letter in the space provided (no punctuation).

   1. ____ disabling
   2. ____ chronic
   3. ____ asymptomatic
   4. ____ acquired
   5. ____ congenital
   6. ____ end-stage
   7. ____ acute
   8. ____ intermittent

   A. illness that is short and relatively severe
   B. disease causing impairment of normal functions
   C. present at birth
   D. symptoms caused at intervals
   E. progressively deteriorating condition
   F. disease the patient is not born with
   G. persisting over a long period of time
   H. having no symptoms

Symptomatic Terms – Lesson 2

I. TERMINOLOGY.
   Enter each term in the space provided. Read the definition and description for each term.

   1. **malignant** _____

   Tending to become progressively worse and eventually causing death. This is usually attributed to types of tumors or cancers but can also describe other problems, such as malignant hypertension.

   2. **neonatal** _____

   Affecting newborns, especially common in prematurely born infants. Neonatal also simply has reference to newborns, not necessarily connoting disease.

   3. **paroxysmal** _____

   A sudden recurrence or intensification of symptoms; a seizure or attack. Paroxysmal nocturnal dyspnea, for example, is a nighttime attack of breathing difficulty.

   4. **progressive** _____

   Advancing, going forward; going from bad to worse; increasing in severity. This is a disease that becomes worse over time. For many people, vision becomes progressively worse throughout their lives.

   5. **recurrent** _____

   Reappears after it has apparently gone away. Cancer patients are consistently rechecked to see if there has been any recurrence after they have stopped showing signs of disease.

   6. **relapsing** _____

   The return of a disease after its apparent cessation. This means basically the same thing as recurrent.

7. **remissive** _____

Most or all of the symptoms have gone away. They can disappear either spontaneously or because of treatment, and the disappearance can be either temporary or permanent.

8. **sequela** _____

A condition resulting from a prior disease, injury, or attack. For example, a sequela of chickenpox.

9. **subacute** _____

Refers to an illness that is neither acute nor chronic, but is somewhere in between.

10. **terminal** _____

Expected to end in death regardless of treatment.

II. **MATCHING.**
   Match the appropriate terms below.

1. ____ sequela
2. ____ progressive
3. ____ neonatal
4. ____ terminal
5. ____ recurrent
6. ____ malignant
7. ____ paroxysmal
8. ____ subacute
9. ____ remissive
10. ____ relapsing

A. recurrence of disease
B. tends to become worse and cause death, i.e. tumor
C. sudden recurrence of symptoms
D. diseases affecting newborns
E. abnormality continues after original disease has resolved
F. disease where most symptoms have gone away
G. disease where death is expected
H. disease reappears after it apparently had gone away
I. increasing in severity
J. illness which is neither acute nor chronic

Unit 3
Anatomy Overview

Anatomy Overview – Introduction

Like a renowned piece of artwork, the human body is a masterpiece of simple cells, microscopic parts, and complex structures that work together for the total being. While the medical practitioner and the medical transcriptionist must have a solid understanding of the human body in order to properly carry out their duties, your knowledge base of human anatomy need not be nearly as complex and intricate as that of a doctor. However, understanding the human body, its parts, and how they complement one another is essential for a career in the profession of medical transcription. After all, it is **you** who will transcribe what the dictator says.

As you work your way through these body structures, you will notice that for every structure there are subdivisions and subcategories associated with each. For example, you will learn that while there are muscles throughout the face and neck, there are specific muscles used for facial expression and chewing. Similarly, there are subdivisions associated with human anatomy. Gross anatomy is the study of macroscopic (large) structures and microscopic anatomy is the study of microscopic (small) structures. Just as the inner mechanisms of a computer are related, whether the CPU processor or the smallest microchip, the human body's structure and function are interrelated as well. The components we will cover in this module include:

If you were planning a career as a computer repair technician, it would be necessary to understand how the parts fit together, what goes where, and how something acts within the inner mechanisms if a problem is suspected or detected. This same adage holds true with knowledge of the human body—having an understanding of what parts make up the human body and the maladies that affect it will serve you greatly as you progress through your career as a medical transcriptionist.

- Muscles
- Arteries
- Veins
- Bones
- Sensory Organs
- Brain

Think of yourself as navigating along the smaller pathways and larger intersections that are the human body. You will charter one structure at a time—learning new terms and understanding the parts that make up the whole. The more you know, the more you can apply to your career in medical transcription. Knowledge truly is power.

Structural Organization

Anatomy refers to the study of the structure of the body. The human body is made up of six levels of structural organization. Each of these levels is related to each other.

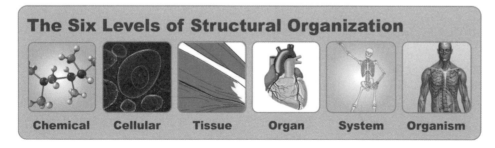

The Six Levels of Structural Organization

Chemical | Cellular | Tissue | Organ | System | Organism

Level	Structure Definition
Chemical	The smallest components. For example, atoms and molecules. Atoms such as nitrogen, oxygen, and calcium are essential to the maintenance of life. These atoms combine to form molecules in the body. Examples of molecules are proteins, carbohydrates, fats, and vitamins.
Cellular	Molecules combine together to form the cellular level. The cells of the body are the basic structural and functional units of an organism. Examples of cells in the body include muscle cells, nerve cells, and blood cells.
Tissue	Tissues are made up of groups of cells and the materials surrounding them. They work together to perform specific functions. There are four types of tissues in your body. The four types of tissue are: • **epithelial** – Protective tissue found in the linings of cavities and organs and as part of the integumentary system, or skin. This tissue helps to protect the structures it lines from injury and fluid loss. • **muscle** – Responsible for all of the movement of the body. It is subdivided into divisions of skeletal muscle, smooth muscle, and cardiac muscle. Skeletal muscle is made of long fibers and is the tissue that allows for voluntary body movements. Smooth muscle lines the internal organs and carries out primarily involuntary body movements that assist in organ function. Cardiac muscle is found only in the heart and is specifically designed to maintain heartbeat and blood flow. • **connective** – Tissue that binds the body together and supports posture and function. This tissue is divided into three subtypes depending on function. Supporting connective tissue consists of the bones and cartilage of the body, which give the body support and base structure. Binding connective tissue is defined as the tendons and ligaments—thick strong tissue that binds muscle to bone and bones to each other. Fibrous connective tissue is also a binding material, though instead of connecting other connective tissues, this tissue connects muscles together and binds the skin to the rest of the body. Adipose, or fat cells, are part of this subdivision serving as a cushioning layer to protect the body. • **nervous** – Composed of nerves and is the communication system of the body, passing electronic messages from the brain. This allows for all motor functions both voluntary and involuntary.
Organ	The different kinds of tissue discussed above combine to form the organ level. The organs are composed of two or more types of these tissues. Each organ has specific functions and recognizable shapes. Some examples of organs are the heart, lungs, brain, liver, and kidneys.
System	A system is made up of several organs that have a common function. For example, the organs that are a part of the digestive system break down and absorb food. These organs include the mouth, pharynx (throat), esophagus, stomach, small intestine, and large intestine. Some organs can be part of more than one system. For example, the pancreas is part of both the digestive system and the endocrine system.
Organism	The largest structural level is the organism level. All the parts which make up the body and function with each other form the total organism (one living individual).

Unit 4
Muscles

Muscles – Introduction

A muscle is an organ that contracts to produce movement in an animal organism. It is this contraction that makes movement possible in human beings. Without muscles, there would be no movement of the body whatsoever. There are two different types of muscles: striated and nonstriated. **Striated** (meaning striped) muscles include both voluntary muscles that respond to nerve signals from the brain to carry out a variety of movements and functions, and the muscles of the heart. Involuntary muscles are called **nonstriated** or smooth muscles. These include the uterus and the muscular layers of the intestines, bladder, blood vessels, etc.

As mentioned, muscles receive their instructions for movement from the nerves. The nerves contain motor fibers which transmit the impulses from the brain and spinal cord and sensory fibers for proprioception (this is a term which means perception regarding movements and positions of the body). Some muscles are attached directly to the periosteum of certain bones, although most muscles are connected indirectly to the bones through connective tissue bands. One of these bands, which is fibrous and cord-like, is called a tendon, and another is the aponeurosis, which is flat, white, and ribbon-like.

Muscles are actually part of the musculoskeletal system (which, of course, means muscles and skeleton). However, a basic understanding of the muscles of the human body will prove extremely beneficial to you in your career as a medical transcriptionist. The muscles and bones of the body are interrelated; in fact, they depend upon each other to carry out their individual functions. There are over 600 skeletal muscles in the human body (most of these are voluntary or striated muscles). The good news is that you do not have to know every single muscle in the body, or even all the voluntary ones, although there are some individual muscles that you should know.

There are three different types of muscle tissue found throughout the human body:

- **skeletal muscle** – The primary muscle used to allow voluntary movement of the body, usually attached to the skeleton by tendons.
- **smooth muscle** – The muscle that lines the walls of internal organs. This muscle is usually short in its strands and allows for the movement of body fluids and waste through the internal systems.
- **cardiac muscle** – This type of muscle is found only in the heart.

The names of muscles are descriptive. Therefore, it will help you to learn them if you have an understanding of how they are named. There are seven primary ways that the names assigned to muscles are derived.

1. **Shape.** Muscle names are often derived from the actual physical shape of the muscle itself or a defining physical characteristic, such as the number of heads that it has.

   - *rhomboideus* – A muscle of the back, shaped like a rhomboid.
   - *triangularis* – A muscle of the face which is triangular in shape.
   - *triceps* – A muscle with three (tri-) heads.
   - *biceps* – A muscle with two (bi-) heads.

2. **Location.** A muscle can be named for its actual location within the body relative to other body structures.

   - *pectoralis* – Chest muscle located within the pectoral girdle.
   - *intercostal* – Muscle located between ribs (literally means between ribs).
   - *abdominis* – Located in the abdominal area.

3. **Attachment.** Many muscles are named for the bones to which they are attached. The muscle name can combine more than one name when more than one bone is involved.

   - *zygomaticus* – Attached to the zygoma (bone of the face).
   - *sternocleidomastoid* – Attached to the sternum, clavicle, and mastoid process of the skull.

4. **Size.** The actual size of the muscle or its relative size to a similar muscle can be used in naming a muscle.

   - *maximus or major* – Both of these terms mean larger or largest.
   - *minimus or minor* – Meaning smaller or smallest.
   - *longus* – Meaning long.
   - *brevis* – Meaning short.

5. **Orientation of fibers.** This is the direction that the individual fibers of a muscle extend.

   - *oblique* – In a slanting or inclined direction.
   - *rectus* – Meaning straight.
   - *transverse* – Meaning across or placed crosswise.

6. **Relative position.** These delineations contain basic directional planes and are used on similar muscles to designate a slightly different orientation. Often a "medial" will have a corresponding "lateral," as, for example, medial meniscus and lateral meniscus (in the knee). An "external" will have a corresponding "internal," such as the internal and external jugular veins. You will have a chance to learn those structures, and many others like them, in subsequent chapters.

   - *lateral* – Something that is farther from the midpoint or to the side.
   - *medial* – Something closer to the middle or the midline.
   - *internal* – Situated or occurring within or on the inside.
   - *external* – Situated or occurring on the outside.

7. **Function.** Muscles are responsible for movement. However, there are several different types of movements, and muscles are often classified according to the actual movement that they produce.

   - *adductor* – Movement to draw toward a medial plane.
   - *extensor* – General term for a muscle that extends a joint.
   - *flexor* – General term for a muscle that flexes a joint.
   - *levator* – A muscle that elevates or lifts an organ or structure.

You will see how these specific name features relate to the muscles themselves shortly. Meanwhile, direct your attention to #6 for a moment. These relative positions are actually used frequently in medical reports. Not only are they used as descriptive words throughout human anatomy, but doctors must describe any findings on a physical examination, within an operative note, or on an x-ray in great detail. In order to achieve clarity of reference, it is necessary for dictators to use standard directional indicators.

Anatomic and Directional Planes

For these points of reference to be standard they must also be uniform. The descriptive terms are all made with reference to what is called the anatomical position. This is a position with the body erect (standing), feet parallel to each other and flat on the floor, eyes directed forward, arms at the sides of the body with the palms facing forward.

In anatomical terms, any veins, muscles, ligaments, bones, tendons, or other structures that utilize one of these descriptive terms will be specifically related to this anatomical position. If you know and can determine for yourself whether something is above, below, in front of, behind, beside, or near another structure, you can be certain that you are using the correct descriptive term.

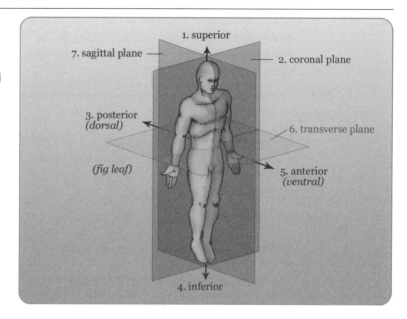

It may be easier for you to learn these terms if you can visualize what the actual directions are. The following exercise will deal with the anatomic planes and directional terms you will use often in medical transcription. Study the terms and complete the exercises. Of note, not all the terms will be depicted in the image.

I. **TERMINOLOGY.**
   Enter each term in the space provided. Read the definition and description for each term.

   1. **anterior** _____

   Situated in front of or toward the front of a body part or organ. Term also used in reference to ventral or belly surface of the body. Frontal is a common synonym for anterior.

   2. **coronal** _____

   Division of the body into anterior and posterior sections. Also called frontal plane. Can mean pertaining to the head or the crown.

   3. **distal** _____

   Remote; farther from the trunk of the body or attachment point; opposite of proximal. (The elbow is proximal to the wrist but distal to the shoulder).

   4. **dorsal** _____

   Pertaining to the back; also used to denote a position that is more toward the back than another object of reference. Sometimes called posterior.

   5. **inferior** _____

   Situated below or directed downward; also used to denote the lower portion of an organ or the lower of two structures. Sometimes called caudal.

6. **lateral** _____

Pertaining to the side; denoting a position farther from the midline (median plane) of a structure.

7. **medial** _____

Pertaining to the middle; closer to the midline of a body; pertaining to the middle layer.

8. **posterior** _____

Situated in the back; also used in reference to the back or dorsal surface of the body.

9. **proximal** _____

Near; closer to the trunk of the body or attachment point; opposite of distal. (The elbow is proximal to the wrist but distal to the shoulder).

10. **sagittal** _____

Division of body into left and right sides in a vertical lengthwise fashion.

11. **transverse** _____

A horizontal plane situated at right angles to the long axis, or sagittal and coronal planes; placed crosswise.

12 **ventral** _____

Pertaining to the abdomen; used to denote a position that is more toward the belly/abdominal surface than some other object of reference.

II. **SPELLING.**
   Determine if the following words are spelled correctly. If the spelling is correct, leave the word as it has already been entered. If the spelling is incorrect, provide the correct spelling.

1. posterior _____   2. ventrol _____

3. dorsal _____   4. choronal _____

5. medial _____   6. latteral _____

7. transverse _____   8. antireor _____

9. saggital _____   10. inferior _____

11. distal _____   12. proximle _____

III. MULTIPLE CHOICE.
Choose the best answer.

1. Placed crosswise.
   - ○ coronal
   - ○ sagittal
   - ⊗ transverse
   - ○ ventral

2. Denoting the lower of two structures.
   - ⊗ inferior
   - ○ superior
   - ○ sagittal
   - ○ coronal

3. Pertaining to the belly side or the abdomen.
   - ○ posterior
   - ⊗ ventral
   - ○ inferior
   - ○ superior

4. Situated in front of.
   - ○ inferior
   - ○ transverse
   - ○ coronalsirology
   - ⊗ anterior

5. Means to the side.
   - ○ medial
   - ⊗ lateral
   - ○ inferior
   - ○ anterior

6. The farthest point.
   - ⊗ distal
   - ○ inferior
   - ○ transverse
   - ○ medial

22

7. The nearest point.
   - ◯ distal
   - ◯ inferior
   - ◯ lateral
   - ⊗ proximal

8. Pertaining to the middle layer.
   - ⊗ medial
   - ◯ lateral
   - ◯ inferior
   - ◯ posterior

9. Pertaining to the head or crown.
   - ⊗ coronal
   - ◯ inferior
   - ◯ superior
   - ◯ transverse

10. Pertaining to the back.
    - ⊗ dorsal
    - ◯ superior
    - ◯ inferior
    - ◯ ventral

11. Toward the belly surface.
    - ◯ coronal
    - ◯ sagittal
    - ⊗ ventral
    - ◯ inferior

12. Situated in back or referencing dorsal surface of body.
    - ⊗ posterior
    - ◯ coronal
    - ◯ sagittal
    - ◯ ventral

Combining Planes

It is often the case that a structure, a mass, or whatever it is that a dictator is referring to is not found precisely in one plane or direction (e.g., anterior or lateral). Instead, the reference is to somewhere between two different planes or directions. In these instances, it is necessary to combine the planes or directions into one word to describe the location (e.g., anterolateral).

You learned in Medical Word Building how to use combining forms. To join directional and positional adjectives, use the combining vowel. Note the following terms that can be joined, their combining forms, and some examples:

Term	Combining Form	Examples
anterior	antero	anteroinferior anterolateral anteromedial anteroposterior
distal	disto	distobuccal distocervical distolabial
dorsal*	dorso	dorsoanterior dorsolateral dorsomedial dorsoposterior
inferior	infero	inferolateral inferomedial inferoposterior
lateral	latero	lateroposition lateroversion
medial	medio	mediocarpal mediolateral
posterior	postero	posteroinferior posterolateral posteromedial
superior	supero	superolateral superomedial
ventral*	ventro	ventrodorsal ventrolateral ventroposterior

*dorso- and ventro- can be designated dorsi- and ventri- in certain instances. However, these forms are generally not used in combination with other positional or anatomical planes. Examples would be dorsiflexion and ventriflexion (which mean bending towards the extensor surface of a limb and bending toward the belly, respectively).

Notice that several of the terms can be combined in both directions, such as inferoposterior and posteroinferior. Fortunately, in transcription you do not have to decide which one should come first, simply transcribe it in the order dictated. You should, however, join terms into one if the dictator says "in the anterior posterior direction." It may be considered incorrect to designate them separately if they are obviously intended as one direction. For example, "in the anterior/posterior direction."

I. **FILL IN THE BLANK.**
   For each problem, join the two terms listed into one word.

   1. ventral + lateral = _ventrolateral_

   2. inferior + posterior = _inferoposterior_

   3. posterior + inferior = _posteroinferior_

   4. superior + lateral = _superolateral_

   5. lateral + posterior = _lateroposterior_

   6. medial + lateral = _mediolateral_

   7. inferior + medial = _inferomedial_

   8. superior + anterior = _superoanterior_

   9. anterior + medial = _anteromedial_

   10. dorsal + flexion = _dorsoflexion_

   11. distal + cervical = _distocervical_

   12. anterior + lateral = _anterolateral_

II. **SPELLING.**
   Determine if the following words are spelled correctly. If the spelling is correct, leave the word as it has already been entered. If the spelling is incorrect, provide the correct spelling.

   1. inferioposterior _____

   2. dorsolateral _____

   3. superioinferior _____

   4. medialateral _____

   5. distobuccal _____

   6. dorsiflexion _____

   7. proximolateral _____

   8. inferomedial _____

   9. superoinferior _____

   10. laterosuperior _____

   11. superiormedial _____

   12. medofrontal _____

III. TRUE/FALSE.
Mark the following true or false.

1. medial + lateral = medialateral

   ◯ true
   ⊗ false

2. distal + cervical = distocervical

   ⊗ true
   ◯ false

3. inferior + posterior = inferiposterior

   ◯ true
   ⊗ false

4. ventral + lateral = ventralateral

   ◯ true
   ⊗ false

5. distal + buccal = distobuccal

   ⊗ true
   ◯ false

6. proximal + lateral = proximolateral

   ⊗ true
   ◯ false

7. dorsal + flexion = dorsiflexion

   ◯ true
   ⊗ false

8. ventral + lateral = ventralateral

   ◯ true
   ⊗ false

Muscles of the Face and Head

Muscles of the face are a very important means of nonverbal communication, as these muscles show fear, anger, surprise, and an array of other emotions. Contracting your facial muscles will elicit a variety of results, depending on the muscle(s) engaged. Note the frontalis muscle in the diagram below—this muscle helps you to frown and also raises your eyebrows. The orbicularis oris is nicknamed the "kissing" muscle because it closes your mouth and puckers your lips when contracting.

The human body has a wide assortment of muscles that permit movement and expression. As you learned with anatomical and directional planes, there are components of these incorporated

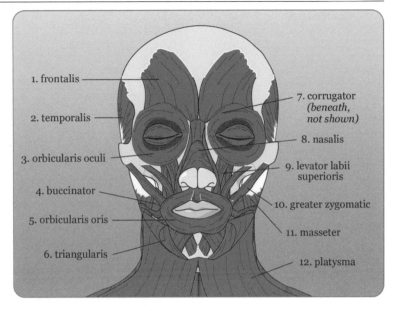

1. frontalis
2. temporalis
3. orbicularis oculi
4. buccinator
5. orbicularis oris
6. triangularis
7. corrugator (beneath, not shown)
8. nasalis
9. levator labii superioris
10. greater zygomatic
11. masseter
12. platysma

into the names of a number of muscles. The following figures are provided as a visual guide. You do not need to memorize and learn each figure in its entirety. Concentrate on the spelling and body placement of the various muscle groups. We will start at the head and work our way down. You will notice some muscles have their attachments in two different areas of the body. For example, the platysma muscle runs from the lower jaw down the neck. It is a muscle of both the face/head and the neck.

I. FILL IN THE BLANK.
Label the muscles of the face and head in the corresponding spaces below. Be sure to spell correctly.

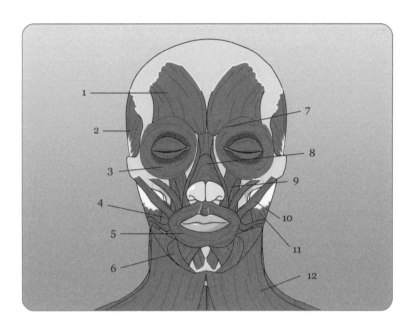

1. FRONTALIS

2. TEMPORALIS

3. ORBICULARIS OCULI

4. BUCCINATOR

5. ORBICULARIS ORIS

6. TRIANGULARIS

7. CORRUGATOR

8. NASALIS

9. LEVATOR LABII SUPERIORIS

10. GREATER ZYGOMATIC

11. MASSETER

12. PLATYSMA

II. MULTIPLE CHOICE.
Choose the term which best describes the statement.

1. The muscle surrounding the eye.

   ○ frontalis
   ○ orbicularis oris
   ○ orbicularis oculi
   ○ orbicularis occuli

2. Lower jaw muscle in the shape of a triangle.

   ○ triangularis
   ○ trangularis
   ○ masseter
   ○ triangularus

3. Muscle located above the eye.

   ○ buccinator
   ○ frontalis
   ○ frontallis
   ○ frontalus

4. Muscle which runs from the lower jaw down the neck.

   ○ platysma
   ○ platisma
   ○ greater zygomatic
   ○ platyssma

5. Cheek muscle.

   ○ bucinator
   ○ temporalis
   ○ buccinater
   ○ buccinator

6. Muscle found in the nose.

   ○ corrugator
   ○ nasalis
   ○ nassalis
   ○ nasales

7. A muscle which lifts and is above the lips.
   - ○ levator labi superioris
   - ○ levator labii superiorus
   - ○ levater labii superioris
   - ○ levator labii superioris

8. Muscle surrounding the mouth.
   - ○ orbicularis oris
   - ○ orbicularis oral
   - ○ orbicularis oculi
   - ○ orbicullaris oris

9. Muscle found in the lower jaw.
   - ○ maseter
   - ○ masseter
   - ○ massetter
   - ○ massiter

10. The larger of the zygomaticus muscles.
    - ○ lesser zygomatic
    - ○ greater zygoma
    - ○ greater zygomatic
    - ○ platysma

11. Muscle located on the side of the head, just above both ears.
    - ○ frontalis
    - ○ temporalis
    - ○ temporallis
    - ○ temperalis

12. Muscle located on the forehead; it creates the "worry lines" or wrinkling of the brow associated with frowning.
    - ○ corrugator
    - ○ corugator
    - ○ corrugater
    - ○ currogator

Muscles of Facial Expression and Mastication

These muscles are primarily used for facial expression and mastication. Mastication is the process of chewing food in preparation for swallowing and digestion. Four pairs of muscles are responsible for the act of mastication or the movement of chewing itself. All four pairs fit into the mandible. This diagram shows muscles that are found deep in the face. These facial muscles will be listed here, along with a brief description.

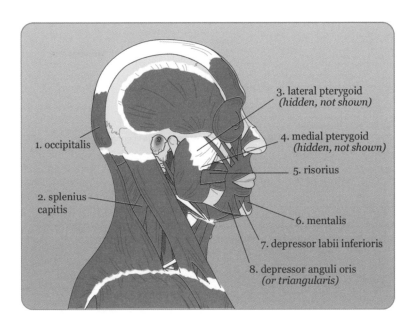

1. occipitalis

2. splenius capitis

3. lateral pterygoid (hidden, not shown)

4. medial pterygoid (hidden, not shown)

5. risorius

6. mentalis

7. depressor labii inferioris

8. depressor anguli oris (or triangularis)

I. **TERMINOLOGY.**
   Enter each term in the space provided. Read the definition and description for each term.

1. **occipitalis** _____

The occipitalis muscle covers the occipital region of the skull.

2. **splenius capitis** _____

This muscle extends from the upper three cervical vertebrae all the way to the temporal and occipital bones. It extends and rotates the head.

3. **lateral pterygoid** _____

This is a muscle of mastication. It originates on the pterygoid process of the sphenoid bone. It moves the mandible and limits sideways jaw movement.

4. **medial pterygoid** _____

Also a muscle of mastication. Both pterygoid muscles are on the inside of the mandible. The medial pterygoid elevates the jaw and provides sideways jaw movement.

5. **risorius** _____

The risorius originates on the side of the face and inserts on the orbicularis oris muscle. It draws the angle of the mouth laterally (to the side) and enables the human being to smile.

6. **mentalis** _____

The mentalis muscle originates on the chin and goes into the orbicularis oris muscle. It elevates and protrudes the lower lip. Basically it allows for pouting.

7. **depressor labii inferioris** _____

This muscle also originates on the mandible and inserts on to the orbicularis muscle. It depresses the bottom lip.
(Names: depressor=depress, labii=lips, inferioris=below or bottom)

8. **depressor anguli oris** _____

This muscle originates on the lower part of the mandible. It pulls down the angle of the mouth.
(Names: depressor=depress, anguli=angle, oris=mouth)

II. **SPELLING.**
   Determine if the following words are spelled correctly. If the spelling is correct, leave the word as it has already been entered. If the spelling is incorrect, provide the correct spelling.

1. ocipitalis _____ 2. mentalis _____

3. capitus _____ 4. terygoid _____

5. labi _____ 6. risorius _____

7. spleenius _____ 8. inferioris _____

Muscles of the Neck

There are many muscles in the neck, but two of the more commonly used muscle terms in medical transcription are *sternocleidomastoid* and *trapezius*. These muscles have counter actions, in that the sternocleidomastoid muscle flexes the neck whereas the trapezius extends the neck.

Muscles of the neck are used to support and move the head. They are also associated with structures found in the neck region, such as the hyoid bone and the larynx. (The larynx is made up of muscle and cartilage, and it both guards the entrance to the trachea and is the voice box.)

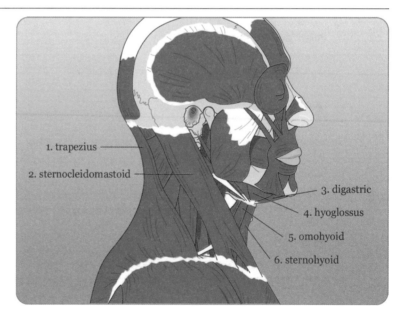

1. trapezius
2. sternocleidomastoid
3. digastric
4. hyoglossus
5. omohyoid
6. sternohyoid

The diagram shows exactly where the structures listed appear. Not all structures can be seen in the angles demonstrated. It is not necessary to memorize this diagram. However, all of the terms that appear were chosen because of their occurrence in medical transcription. If you transcribe reports that deal with this part of the body (and you likely will in some way, shape, or form), you will see these terms often. Again, our emphasis in anatomy is on spelling and a general familiarity with these terms. Please become familiar with the terms shown on the diagram and complete the following exercise.

I. FILL IN THE BLANK.
Label the muscles of the neck in the corresponding spaces below. Be sure to spell correctly.

1. _____   2. _____

3. _____   4. _____

5. _____   6. _____

II. SPELLING.
Determine if the following words are spelled correctly. If the spelling is correct, leave the word as it has already been entered. If the spelling is incorrect, provide the correct spelling.

1. omohyloid _____   2. trapezium _____

3. sternoclidomastoid _____   4. digastric _____

5. hyoglosus _____   6. sternohyoid _____

III. **TRUE/FALSE.**
   The following words are spelled correctly: true or false?

1. hyoglosus
   ○ true
   ○ false

2. dygastric
   ○ true
   ○ false

3. trapezius
   ○ true
   ○ false

4. omohioid
   ○ true
   ○ false

5. sternocleidomastoid
   ○ true
   ○ false

Muscles of the Torso and Back

The muscles and terms found on the following figures are for the superficial muscles of the torso and back. There are many additional muscles located in these regions of the body. If you come across a term that is not delineated below, look in your medical dictionary to find it.

The linea alba and umbilicus are labeled in the figure below; however, they are not muscles. Since they are terms that you will use often in medical transcription, we have included them here for you to identify where they are and how to spell them. Linea alba means literally "white line" and is the term for the tendinous line down the middle of the anterior abdominal wall directly between the two rectus muscles. The umbilicus, as annotated, is the belly button. Notice the term *lumbar aponeurosis*. This is also not a muscle. An aponeurosis, as previously stated, is a white, flattened tendinous expansion, serving mainly to connect a muscle with the parts that it moves. It replaces what were formerly called fasciae (plural), although some doctors and dictators may still use the old terminology. Both names are included in the figure.

34

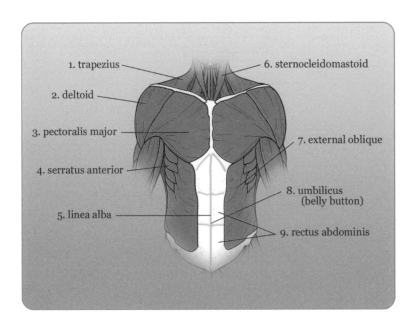

1. trapezius
6. sternocleidomastoid
2. deltoid
3. pectoralis major
7. external oblique
4. serratus anterior
8. umbilicus (belly button)
5. linea alba
9. rectus abdominis

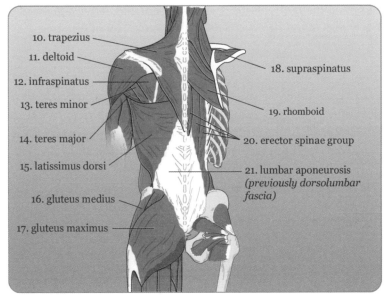

10. trapezius
11. deltoid
12. infraspinatus
13. teres minor
14. teres major
15. latissimus dorsi
16. gluteus medius
17. gluteus maximus
18. supraspinatus
19. rhomboid
20. erector spinae group
21. lumbar aponeurosis *(previously dorsolumbar fascia)*

I. FILL IN THE BLANK.
Label the superficial muscles of the torso and back in the corresponding spaces below. Be sure to spell correctly.

1. _____   2. _____

3. _____   4. _____

5. _____   6. _____

7. _____   8. _____

9. _____   10. _____

11. _____   12. _____

13. _____   14. _____

15. _____   16. _____

17. _____   18. _____

19. _____   20. _____

21. _____

II. SPELLING.

Determine if the following words are spelled correctly. If the spelling is correct, leave the word as it has already been entered. If the spelling is incorrect, provide the correct spelling.

1. line alba _____   2. umbilicis _____

3. pectoralis _____   4. seratus _____

5. abominus _____   6. oblique _____

7. delltoid _____   8. trapezius _____

9. glutues _____   10. romboid _____

III. MULTIPLE CHOICE.

Determine which of the following is correctly spelled in each.

1. Muscle that controls curvature of the lower spine.

   ○ rectus abdominus
   ○ rectus abdominis
   ○ rectis abdominus
   ○ rectis abdominis

2. Muscle that rotates the arm medially.

   ○ teres major
   ○ teris major
   ○ terres major
   ○ terus major

3. A white, flattened, tendinous expansion.

   ○ lumbar aponurosis
   ○ lumbar aponewrosis
   ○ lumbar aponeurrosis
   ○ lumbar aponeurosis

4. Group of posterior spinal column muscles.

   ○ errector spinae
   ○ erector spinae
   ○ erector spinnae
   ○ erector spine

5. Muscle that connects the scapula with the vertebrae.

   ○ rhomboid
   ○ romboid
   ○ rhombiod
   ○ romboide

6. Also called the rotator cuff.

   ○ infraspinatus
   ○ infraspinatis
   ○ infraspinatius
   ○ inferspinatus

7. Muscle that works to move the neck in several directions.

   ○ trepezius
   ○ trapezius
   ○ trapezuis
   ○ trapeziuis

8. The widest and most powerful muscle of the back.

   ○ latissimis dorsi
   ○ latissemus dorsi
   ○ latisimus dorsi
   ○ latissimus dorsi

Muscles of the Arm

Thenar is a term that refers to the mound on the palm at the base of the thumb and also means pertaining to the palm. The terms *hypothenar* and *thenar muscles* describe simply the location of the muscles and are not the name of individual muscles. You should be able to recognize several muscle names in the arm that are descriptive; for example, you should know terms such as *longus* and *brevis* (long and short) and *radialis* and *ulnaris* (for the radius and ulna bones). Also, some of these muscles should be easy because they are so commonly known (e.g., the biceps and triceps).

Note the term *flexor retinaculum*. A retinaculum (plural: retinacula) is a structure that holds an organ or tissue in place. (In surgery, it is also used to describe an instrument that retracts tissues.) As with the aponeurosis, this is not a muscle. It is, however, a significant structure of the arm, and it is important in the musculoskeletal system. Therefore, you should memorize its spelling and be able to recognize it when you hear it dictated.

It may be helpful to start looking for consistencies in the spelling of muscle terms that would make it easier to remember how to spell them. For example, the bones of the forearm are the radius and ulna. The muscles which attach to these bones are named for them; for example, radialis, ulnaris, and brachioradialis. All of these terms end in *is*. Look for these similarities and use them as tools for learning the terms. You will discover that many muscles (although not all of them) end in *is*. It may be easier to learn the exceptions than to memorize each individual term. Of course, if you happened to study Latin along the way, these terms will be simple to learn.

Another feature of muscle terms is that some of them end in *s*, but are not plural. There is no such word as bicep or tricep. The actual definitions for biceps and triceps are literally muscles with two and three heads, respectively. When speaking about these muscles and transcribing them, it should always be biceps and triceps, even in the singular. These are primarily the superficial muscles of the arm. There are other muscles (besides the coracobrachialis and the brachialis) that are located deep. Many of them are identified by terms similar to those listed on the figure. Direct your attention to the term *pollicis*. This is derived from the word *pollex*, which means the first digit of the hand (or for lay-people, the thumb). The muscles that act to move the thumb contain the term *pollicis*. In addition to the abductor pollicis brevis, there is an adductor pollicis, an extensor pollicis, and so on. If you can remember that *pollex* means thumb, you can be sure to use *pollicis* in reference to certain muscles in the hand.

When you learn the muscles of the leg you will see the term *hallux*, which is the great toe (or more commonly, the big toe). Muscles that act to move the big toe are denoted by the term *hallucis*, which is derived from *hallux*. As with *carpals/metacarpals* and *tarsals/metatarsals*, it is easy to confuse the terms *hallux* and *pollex* (and likewise *hallucis* and *pollicis*). Learn the root terms, and it will be easier to delineate between the two words so you can be certain you are using the right one.

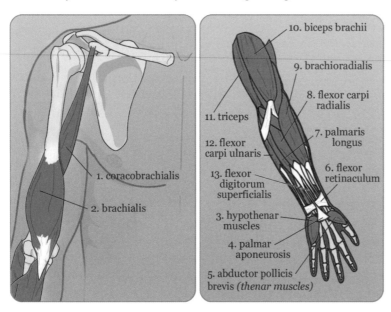

10. biceps brachii
9. brachioradialis
8. flexor carpi radialis
11. triceps
7. palmaris longus
12. flexor carpi ulnaris
6. flexor retinaculum
1. coracobrachialis
13. flexor digitorum superficialis
2. brachialis
3. hypothenar muscles
4. palmar aponeurosis
5. abductor pollicis brevis *(thenar muscles)*

I. FILL IN THE BLANK.
Label the muscles of the arm in the corresponding spaces below. Be sure to spell correctly.

1. _____   2. _____

3. _____   4. _____

5. _____   6. _____

7. _____   8. _____

9. _____   10. _____

11. _____   12. _____

13. _____

II. SPELLING.
Determine if the following words are spelled correctly. If the spelling is correct, leave the word as it has already been entered. If the spelling is incorrect, provide the correct spelling.

1. choracobrachialis _____   2. bicep _____

3. ulnaris _____   4. brevis _____

5. brachialus _____   6. hypothenor _____

7. palmer _____   8. policis _____

9. digitorum _____   10. flexer _____

11. abductor _____   12. tricep _____

Actions of Arm Muscles

The arm and hand muscles are most commonly transcribed in radiology (x-ray) reports, orthopedics (especially operative notes), and physical therapy, although, as with other terms, they might turn up virtually anywhere. It is important for you to begin to recognize the terms for the muscles associated with the hand that indicate position and movement, as well as more basic body location: supinate, pronate, flex, extend, digits, pollex, for example. The more you understand what you are transcribing, the more accurate and professional your work will eventually be. Lucky for you, you do **not** have to memorize exactly what each one of these muscles does.

Located below are a few of the muscles that are located beneath the muscles shown in the previous figures.

I. **TERMINOLOGY.**
   Enter each term in the space provided. Read the definition and description for each term.

   1. **anconeus** _____

   Located on the back of the humerus, it extends the forearm.

   2. **extensor digiti minimi** _____

   A long narrow muscle located on the ulnar side of the extensor digitorum communis muscle. It assists in extension of the wrist and little finger.

   3. **extensor digitorum communis** _____

   Positioned in the center of the forearm along the posterior surface. Its tendon divides into four tendons beneath the extensor retinaculum, which attach to the distal tips of fingers one through four.

   4. **flexor digitorum profundus** _____

   Lies just underneath the flexor digitorum superficialis muscle. This muscle flexes the distal ends of the fingers (but not the thumb).

   5. **flexor pollicis longus** _____

   Positioned deep on the front of the radius. It attaches at the base of the thumb and flexes the thumb and makes grasping possible.

   6. **pronator teres** _____

   Positioned in upper middle part of the forearm. It arises from the **epicondyle** (a prominence or projection on a bone). It turns the hand downwards (called pronation) and flexes the elbow.

   7. **epicondyle** _____

   A prominence or projection on a bone.

8. **pronator quadratus** _____

Positioned deep and extends between the ulna and radius. It works with the other pronator muscle to rotate the palm of the hand down, as well as position the thumb medially.

9. **supinator** _____

Positioned around the upper portion of the radius. It works with the biceps to turn the palm upwards (called supination).

II. MULTIPLE CHOICE.
Choose the term which best describes the statement.

1. To extend the palm upwards.

    ◯ suppinate
    ⊗ supinate
    ◯ pronate
    ◯ suepinate

2. The first digit of the hand (the thumb).

    ◯ hallux
    ◯ polex
    ⊗ pollex
    ◯ carpals

3. Located behind the humerus and extends the forearm.

    ⊗ anconeus
    ◯ anconius
    ◯ anconeis
    ◯ anconneus

4. Long narrow muscle which assists in extension of the wrist and little finger.

    ◯ extensor digitus minimus
    ⊗ extensor digiti minimi
    ◯ extensor digiti mimini
    ◯ extensor digitus maximus

5. Another term for palmar.

    ◯ tenar
    ◯ theno
    ⊗ thenar
    ◯ thennar

6. Descriptive muscle term meaning short.
   - ◯ longus
   - ◯ brevus
   - ◯ brives
   - ⊗ brevis

7. Muscle attached to the humerus deep to the biceps.
   - ⊗ coracobrachialis
   - ◯ coracobrachialus
   - ◯ coronobrachialis
   - ◯ chorobrachialis

8. A structure which holds an organ or a tissue in place.
   - ◯ aponeurosis
   - ⊗ retinaculum
   - ◯ retinaculim
   - ◯ apponeurosis

9. The major muscle of the upper arm.
   - ◯ bicep
   - ◯ flexor carpi ulnaris
   - ⊗ biceps
   - ◯ bicepps

10. A muscle which turns the palm of the hand downwards.
    - ◯ pronater teres
    - ⊗ pronator teres
    - ◯ pronator terres
    - ◯ pronater teris

11. A muscle whose tendon divides into four different tendons.
    - ◯ extensor digitorum comminus
    - ◯ extensor digiti comminus
    - ⊗ extensor digitorum communis
    - ◯ extensor digiti communis

12. Long slender arm muscle with a tendon which attaches to the palmar aponeurosis.
    - ⊗ palmaris longus
    - ◯ palmaris brevis
    - ◯ palmarus longis
    - ◯ palmaris longis

13. Muscle located on the back of the arm.

- ○ tricep
- ○ thenar muscle
- ○ bicep
- ⊗ triceps

14. Muscle which flexes the fingers.

- ○ flesor digitorum profundis
- ⊗ flexor digitorum profundus
- ○ extensor digiti profundidi
- ○ flexor digotorum profundus

Muscles of the Leg

In medical transcription, the legs are rarely referred to as such; they are instead referred to as the lower extremities. (The arms are likewise called the upper extremities.) An extremity is simply the name for a limb. You should notice, as with the arm muscles, there will be descriptive terms in the diagrams that should be familiar by now, such as *longus, brevis, hallucis,* and *maximus.* Take just a moment to find any terms that you already know.

There are also a few terms listed on this image that are not muscles, although they are vital to the musculoskeletal system—especially the lower extremities. The lateral malleolus refers to the ankle bone on the outside of the ankle joint, formed by the distal end of the fibula; the medial malleolus refers to the ankle bone on the inside of the ankle joint, formed by the distal end of the tibia. The term *medial*, in this case does not refer to the middle of the ankle joint itself, but is only a directional term indicating the structure is nearer the midline of the body. When you hold your feet very close together the two medial malleoli touch.

The second term is the *calcaneal*, or Achilles tendon. It is the thickest and strongest tendon in the body. You have already learned that tendons are fibrous cords by which muscle is attached. (If you are into mythology, the Achilles tendon is named for the Greek fighter Achilles. He was immortal and invulnerable except for the spot on his heel where he was held as he was dipped into the river water which turns mortals into gods. It was this area that was pierced by an arrow during the Trojan War, and this wound caused his death.)

The extensor retinaculum covers and holds in place the muscles and tendons of the front of the foot. The tibia is a bone. The greater trochanter, also called trochanter major, is a broad, flat process to which several muscles are attached. Finally, the iliotibial tract is a thick, long band of fascia lata that extends down the side of the thigh to the tibia.

All of these terms will come up frequently in medical transcription, and you should be able to recognize and spell them.

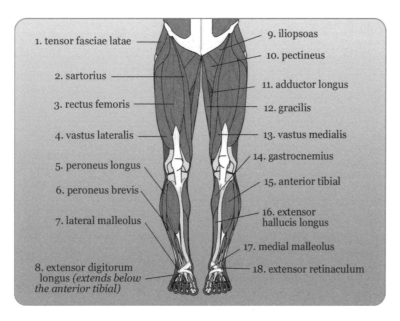

1. tensor fasciae latae
2. sartorius
3. rectus femoris
4. vastus lateralis
5. peroneus longus
6. peroneus brevis
7. lateral malleolus
8. extensor digitorum longus *(extends below the anterior tibial)*
9. iliopsoas
10. pectineus
11. adductor longus
12. gracilis
13. vastus medialis
14. gastrocnemius
15. anterior tibial
16. extensor hallucis longus
17. medial malleolus
18. extensor retinaculum

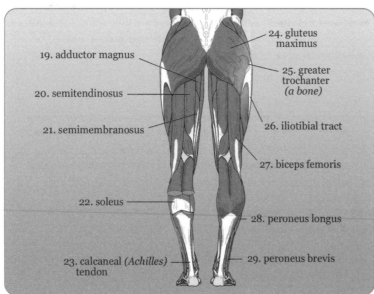

19. adductor magnus
20. semitendinosus
21. semimembranosus
22. soleus
23. calcaneal *(Achilles)* tendon
24. gluteus maximus
25. greater trochanter *(a bone)*
26. iliotibial tract
27. biceps femoris
28. peroneus longus
29. peroneus brevis

I. FILL IN THE BLANK.
Enter the appropriate leg muscles of the corresponding numbers in the boxes below.

1. _____   2. _____

3. _____   4. _____

5. _____   6. _____

7. _____   8. _____

9. _____   10. _____

11. _____   12. _____

13. _____   14. _____

15. _____   16. _____

17. _____   18. _____

19. _____   20. _____

21. _____   22. _____

23. _____   24. _____

25. _____   26. _____

27. _____   28. _____

29. _____

II. **SPELLING.**
Determine if the following words are spelled correctly. If the spelling is correct, leave the word as it has already been entered. If the spelling is incorrect, provide the correct spelling.

1. maleolus _MALLEOLUS_   2. fasciae _✓_

3. lateralis _✓_   4. longus _✓_

5. gastrocnemis _GASTROCNEMIUS_ 6. halucis _HALLUCIS_

7. maximus _✓_   8. semitendonosis _SEMITENDINOSUS_

9. achilles _✓_   10. extensor _✓_

III. **TRUE/FALSE.**
Determine if the following statements are true or false.

1. The extensor retinaculum is an anterior muscle of the leg.

   ◯ true
   ⊗ false

2. Peroneus brevis is spelled correctly.

   ⊗ true
   ◯ false

3. Iliotibeal tract is spelled correctly.

   ○ true
   ⊗ false

4. The gluteus maximus is a posterior muscle.

   ⊗ true
   ○ false

5. Another name for the Achilles tendon is the soleus tendon.

   ○ true
   ⊗ false

6. Vastis lateralis is spelled correctly.

   ○ true
   ⊗ false

7. Tensor fasciae latae is spelled correctly.

   ⊗ true
   ○ false

8. Peroneus longus is an anterior muscle while peroneus brevis is a posterior muscle.

   ○ true
   ⊗ false

IV. MULTIPLE CHOICE.
Choose the best answer.

1. This is a fascial structure of the leg.

   ○ extensor retonaculum
   ⊗ extensor retinaculum
   ○ extensor retenaculum
   ○ extensir retinaculum

2. This is a hip flexor.

   ○ ileopsoas
   ○ iliosoas
   ○ eliopsoas
   ⊗ iliopsoas

3. This muscle includes both a long and a short.

   ○ byceps
   ⊗ biceps
   ○ bieceps
   ○ byceeps

4. This is an anterior leg muscle.

   ○ rectis femoris
   ⊗ rectus femoris
   ○ rectis femorus
   ○ rectus femurus

5. Muscle located at the back and medial side of the thigh.

   ⊗ semimembranosus
   ○ semimembranosis
   ○ semimembrainosus
   ○ semimembrainosis

Review: Muscles

You have flexed and extended many of your own body's muscles as you have worked through this unit. Now supinate your palm, flex your shoulder until your hand is on your scapula, and pat yourself on the back for a job well done! These are the muscles and related terms that you should know how to spell. You should also know approximately where they are in the body. You will not be tested now or later on exactly which muscle is which, and you will not be required to label any figures studied in this unit.

I. **SPELLING.**
   Determine if the following words are spelled correctly. If the spelling is correct, leave the word as it has already been entered. If the spelling is incorrect, provide the correct spelling.

   1. striated _____✓_____   2. pterigoid _PTERYGOID_

   3. superficialus _SUPERFICIALIS_   4. anguli _____✓_____

   5. latissimis _LATISSIMUS_   6. halucis _HALLUCIS_

   7. infraspinatous _INFRASPINATUS_   8. digitorim _DIGITORUM_

   9. corugator _CORRUGATOR_   10. platysma _____✓_____

47

II. FILL IN THE BLANK.
Determine where in the body the muscle is found. Choose from the following list and enter the correct part of the body in the space provided.

1. mentalis _____f/h_____
2. biceps _____a_____
3. anconeus _____a_____
4. palmaris longus _____a_____
5. splenius capitis _____f/h_____
6. medial pterygoid _____f/h_____
7. masseter _____f/h_____
8. omohyoid _____n_____
9. anterior tibial _____l_____
10. external oblique _____t/t_____

| face/head |
| arm |
| trunk/torso |
| neck |
| leg |

III. MULTIPLE CHOICE.
Choose the term which best describes the statement.

1. The forearm muscle which pronates the hand.
   - ○ anconeus
   - ○ pronater teres
   - ⊗ pronator teres
   - ○ pronator terres

2. A long narrow muscle which assists in extending the wrist and little finger.
   - ○ extensor digiti minimus
   - ⊗ extensor digiti minimi
   - ○ extensor digitii mimini
   - ○ flexorum digiti minimi

3. The major superficial muscle of the shoulder.
   - ⊗ deltoid
   - ○ delltoid
   - ○ gluteus maximus
   - ○ soleus

48

4. The responsibility of this muscle is to aid in chewing.
    - ⊗ lateral pterygoid
    - ◯ lateral pterigoid
    - ◯ medial pteromogoid
    - ◯ medial pterycept

5. Bony prominence on the side of the ankle joint.
    - ◯ lateral maleolus
    - ⊗ lateral malleolus
    - ◯ greater trochanter
    - ◯ sagittal malleolus

6. Abdominal muscle.
    - ⊗ external oblique
    - ◯ external obliquis
    - ◯ Achilles tendon
    - ◯ linea obliquus

7. Process on the outer thigh to which several muscles are attached.
    - ◯ greater trocanter
    - ◯ greater trochantor
    - ⊗ greater trochanter
    - ◯ greater trockanter

8. Muscle of the back of the leg.
    - ◯ semimembranosis
    - ⊗ semimembranosus
    - ◯ semimembrainosus
    - ◯ semimembrinosus

9. The term for perception regarding movements and positions of the body.
    - ◯ propreoception
    - ◯ preproception
    - ⊗ proprioception
    - ◯ proprioseption

10. A muscle of the skull.
    - ⊗ occipitalis
    - ◯ ocipitalis
    - ◯ occipitalus
    - ◯ occipitallis

Muscle Disease Processes – Introduction

As you know, a ligament is a band of connective tissue joining bone to bone. Think of it this way: B L B (bone–ligament–bone). Without the ligament, you'd be a "blob." Clever puns aside, muscles themselves become a blob of sorts and do not function properly or as they should when disease strikes.

There are literally hundreds of problems that can affect the muscles. Because of the sheer volume of these individual muscular processes, we will be focusing on more general problems and disease processes that afflict muscles. A medical dictionary (online or hard copy) will be a valuable tool in referencing any individual terms that you come across in this section.

As with any other part of the human anatomy, the muscles, their attachments, and associated structures can be injured, infected, diseased, or deformed. Minor muscle injuries are usually diagnosed and treated by family practice doctors. They are also routinely treated in emergency rooms and clinics. More serious injuries or disease processes affecting the muscles will be managed by orthopedists and orthopedic surgeons.

Muscle Disease Processes – Lesson 1

Many of the disease processes are created with combining forms. For example, the combining form for muscle is *my/o*. The suffix that means pain is *-algia*. Therefore, muscle pain is myalgia.

The exercises that follow are designed to better acquaint you with muscular disease terminology that you might encounter as a medical transcriptionist.

   I. **TERMINOLOGY.**
       Enter each term in the space provided. Read the definition and description for each term.

        1. **atony** _____

        Lack of normal tone or strength. This happens in muscles that are deprived of innervation. Try not to confuse this term with atrophy (below) or atopy (which is a genetic predisposition towards hypersensitivity to common environmental antigens).

        2. **atrophy** _____

        The wasting away or weakening of muscle fibers due to a lack of usage. There are many different kinds of atrophy. Look up *atrophy* in a medical dictionary and read or scan the terms which appear under this category.

        3. **bursitis** _____

        Inflammation of a bursa.

        4. **bursa** _____

        A sac-like cavity filled with synovial fluid that is located in places where tendons or muscles pass over bony prominences.

        5. **charley horse** _____

        A bruised or torn muscle accompanied by cramps and severe pain. This particular injury most commonly affects the quadriceps muscle. (Incidentally, quadriceps is like biceps or triceps and always has the *s*," whether singular or plural.) Lay people refer to any muscle spasm of the legs or feet as a charley horse.

6. **cramp** _____

A sustained spasm or contraction of a muscle accompanied by severe, localized pain.

7. **dystonia** _____

Sustained abnormal postures or disruptions of normal movement resulting from alterations of muscle tone.

8. **Dupuytren's contracture** _____

Painless thickening and contracture of the palmar fascia due to fibrous proliferation, resulting in loss of function of the fingers.

9. **fasciculations** _____

Similar to fibrillations or tremors. A repetitive, involuntary contraction of muscle. The main cause is nerve damage.

10. **fibromyalgia** _____

A group of rheumatic disorders characterized by achy pain, tenderness, and stiffness of muscles and tendon insertions. (Also called myofascial pain syndrome and fibromyositis.)

Muscle Disease Processes – Lesson 2

I. **TERMINOLOGY.**
   Enter each term in the space provided. Read the definition and description for each term.

1. **myofascial pain syndrome** _____

A chronic condition affecting the fascia, or connective tissue covering muscles. It may involve a single muscle or muscle group.

2. **fibromyositis** _____

The chronic inflammation of a muscle with hyperplasia (overgrowth) of connective tissue.

3. **ganglion** _____

A thin-walled band cyst formed on a joint capsule or tendon sheath.

4. **leiomyoma** _____

A benign tumor of smooth muscle tissue, e.g., the uterus.

5. **muscular dystrophy** _____

A genetic abnormality of muscle tissue characterized by dysfunction and ultimately deterioration.

6. **myalgia** _____

Muscle pain.

7. **myasthenia gravis** _____

A chronic progressive neuromuscular weakness, usually starting with the muscles of the face and throat.

8. **myopathy** _____

Any disease of the muscles.

9. **myositis ossificans** _____

A disease characterized by bony deposits or the ossification of muscle tissue.

10. **paralysis** _____

The loss of nervous control of a muscle. This impairment is commonly thought of as related to paraplegia or quadriplegia. However, there are many different types of paralysis affecting many different muscles and organs of the body. These can be seen in a medical dictionary under _paralysis_.

Muscle Disease Processes – Lesson 3

I. **TERMINOLOGY.**
   Enter each term in the space provided. Read the definition and description for each term.

1. **paraplegia** _____

Paralysis of the legs (lower extremities).

2. **quadriplegia** _____

Paralysis of all four limbs.

3. **plantar fasciitis** _____

Excessive pulling or stretching of the calcaneal periosteum by the plantar fascia, resulting in pain along the inner border of the plantar fascia. This definition applies specifically to the process which affects the plantar surface of the foot. Fasciitis is inflammation of the fascia. There are other types of fasciitis, which can be seen in a medical dictionary under _fasciitis_.

4. **polymyositis** _____

An autoimmune disorder which causes atrophy and weakness of the muscles.

5. **rigor mortis** _____

Rigor means chilled, stiffness, rigidity. Rigor mortis is the muscular hardness occurring four to seven hours after death.

6. **tendinitis** _____

Inflammation of a tendon or the synovial lining of a tendon sheath due to trauma or repetitive wear. (Note the spelling. Tendonitis is an acceptable alternative spelling, but tendinitis is preferred.)

7. **tenosynovitis** _____

The inflammation of the tendon and the tendon sheath.

8. **tennis elbow** _____

A strain of the lateral forearm muscles or the tendinous attachments near their origin on the epicondyle of the humerus.

9. **lateral and medial epicondylitis** _____

Also referred to as tennis elbow, a condition characterized by weakness and pain in the muscles and tendons of the outside elbow.

10. **tetanus** _____

A disease caused by the bacterium Clostridium tetani, which produces a toxin that causes muscles to go into tetany (hyperexcitability of nerves and muscles, specifically characterized by muscular cramps and twitching). Jaw muscles are affected first. Lockjaw is the more common name.

11. **torticollis** _____

Contraction of sternocleidomastoid muscle, causing rotation of the head.

Disorders Affecting the Muscular System

Several brain function or neurological problems manifest themselves through the muscles, taking the form of abnormal muscular movements. For example, a **seizure** is a sudden attack of a disease, but is commonly thought of in reference to epilepsy. **Epilepsy** is any of a group of syndromes that are characterized by a disturbance in brain function, which results in loss of consciousness, abnormal motor phenomena, or neurosensory disturbances. An episode resulting from an epileptic condition is called a seizure.

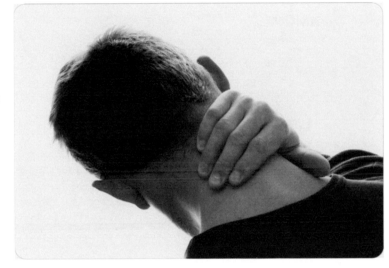

Abnormal motor phenomena are manifested in the muscular system. A common type of abnormal motor activity is clonic activity. Clonic is the adjectival form of clonus; **clonus** is alternate muscular contraction and relaxation in rapid succession. Clonic is a term generally used in conjunction with the term **tonic**, which means normal tone. So, during a seizure it is often the case that the muscles go through a series of rapid contractions alternating with a return to normal muscle tone. This movement is called tonic-clonic activity or tonicoclonic activity. Although it is not actually caused by an injury to or defect in the muscles themselves, it undoubtedly affects the muscular system.

Another common neurologic disorder that affects the muscular system is **Parkinson disease**. This is a progressive degenerative nervous system disorder that is characterized by four features: slowness and absence of movement, muscular rigidity, resting tremor, and unstable posture. **Rigidity** means stiffness or inflexibility. This is the fourth most common disease afflicting the elderly. Again, while the cause of the disorder is neurological, all of the manifestations are musculoskeletal.

Muscle tissue makes up a major part of the human body. Of course, there are many more muscles and disease processes of muscles than are covered in this session. However, we have hit upon the most common terms.

I. TRUE/FALSE.
The following words are spelled correctly: true or false?

1. paralysis
   - ○ true
   - ○ false

2. epicondilitis
   - ○ true
   - ○ false

3. bursytis
   - ○ true
   - ○ false

4. tetanus
   - ○ true
   - ○ false

5. rigidity
   - ○ true
   - ○ false

6. polymiositis
   - ○ true
   - ○ false

7. tendenitis
   - ○ true
   - ○ false

8. Parkinsen
   - ○ true
   - ○ false

II. MATCHING.
Match the appropriate terms below.

1. ____ Charley horse
2. ____ tonic/clonic
3. ____ tetanus
4. ____ atrophy
5. ____ rigor mortis
6. ____ myasthenia gravis
7. ____ leiomyoma
8. ____ bursa

A. a disease caused by bacteria
B. a chronic progressive neuromuscular weakness
C. a bruised or torn muscle which particularly affects the quadriceps muscle
D. a sac-like cavity filled with synovial fluid and located over bony prominences
E. muscle response to seizure activity
F. a benign tumor of smooth muscle
G. wasting away or weakening of muscles
H. the muscular hardness of death

III. MULTIPLE CHOICE.
Choose the term which best describes the statement.

1. Pain in a muscle.
   - ○ myalgia
   - ○ myagia
   - ○ myositis
   - ○ mylagia

2. Contraction of sternocleidomastoid muscle, causing rotation of the head.
   - ○ torticolis
   - ○ tortocolis
   - ○ torticollis
   - ○ torticolus

3. A nervous system disorder characterized by four muscular features.
   - ○ Parkonson disease
   - ○ Parkinson disease
   - ○ Parkenson disease
   - ○ Parkenson disease

4. A cyst on a joint capsule or tendon sheath.
   - ⭕ ganglion
   - ⭕ gangleon
   - ⭕ ganglius
   - ⭕ gangliona

5. Another name for tremors.
   - ⭕ fasciculations
   - ⭕ fasiculations
   - ⭕ fascisulations
   - ⭕ faciculations

Unit 5
Arteries

Arteries of the Head, Neck, and Brain

Arteries are muscular blood vessels that carry blood away from the heart. As you have learned in the lessons on muscles, contraction and expansion are key muscular functions. Arteries are both tough and elastic in order to transport blood away from the heart. As you take this journey into arteries, do not become overwhelmed with the material presented—take it one page at a time. Slow and steady wins the race.

Blood begins its course throughout the body in the arteries. We will start at the top of the body and work our way down. Be aware, however, that the veins and arteries branch from the center outward, upward, and downward, and therefore the largest structures are those closest to the heart itself. This is discussed in greater detail later in this unit. The terms that you will be learning in the rest of this unit are by no means all of the arteries and veins in the body. However, you should have a much better idea of the major arteries, which are the most likely ones to be affected by procedures and operations and to show up on x-rays. Of course, the greater your exposure to and familiarity with the most commonly used terms, the easier it will be for you to search out the ones that are used only rarely.

Again, most structures of the body that have an *inferior* have a corresponding *superior* that may not be listed. You should also take notice of terms such as ophthalmic, which means pertaining to the eye, and auricular, which means pertaining to the ear, to help you understand the artery location and function.

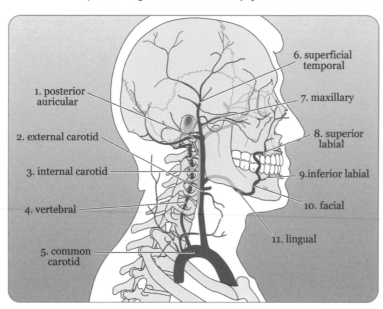

1. posterior auricular
2. external carotid
3. internal carotid
4. vertebral
5. common carotid
6. superficial temporal
7. maxillary
8. superior labial
9. inferior labial
10. facial
11. lingual

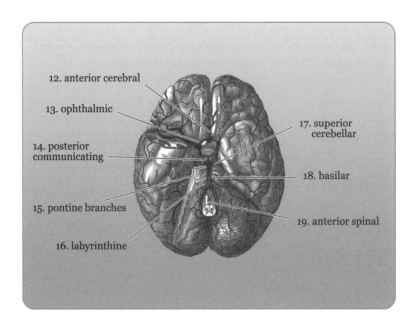

12. anterior cerebral

13. ophthalmic

14. posterior communicating

15. pontine branches

16. labyrinthine

17. superior cerebellar

18. basilar

19. anterior spinal

I. **FILL IN THE BLANK.**
   Label the arteries of the head, neck, and brain in the corresponding spaces below. Be sure to spell them correctly.

1. _____   2. _____

3. _____   4. _____

5. _____   6. _____

7. _____   8. _____

9. _____   10. _____

11. _____   12. _____

13. _____   14. _____

15. _____   16. _____

17. _____   18. _____

19. _____

II. SPELLING.
Determine if the following words are spelled correctly. If the spelling is correct, leave the word as it has already been entered. If the spelling is incorrect, provide the correct spelling.

1. basillar _____

2. cerebellar _____

3. opthalmic _____

4. vertebral _____

5. cerebral _____

6. inferior _____

7. labeal _____

8. fascial _____

9. labryinthine _____

10. auricular _____

11. lingual _____

12. carotid _____

13. pontin _____

14. branches _____

15. comunicating _____

III. MULTIPLE CHOICE.
Choose the term which best describes the statement.

1. A term meaning pertaining to the eye.
   ○ opthalmic
   ○ ophthalmic
   ○ ophtalmic
   ○ auricular

2. The artery which passes through the vertebrae.
   ○ vertebral
   ○ vetebral
   ○ verterbral
   ○ veterbral

3. The artery which runs in the front of the face.
   ○ fascial
   ○ vertebral
   ○ facial
   ○ faceal

4. Branches of the basilar artery.
   ○ pontine
   ○ pantine
   ○ Pantene
   ○ pontene

5. Arteries above and below the lips.
   ○ labeal
   ○ labial
   ○ labbial
   ○ ophthalmic

6. Means pertaining to the ear.
   ○ auricular
   ○ aricular
   ○ aurecular
   ○ auriculaur

7. Runs through the internal acoustic meatus to the internal ear.
   ○ labyrinth
   ○ labyrinthine
   ○ labryinthine
   ○ labirynthine

8. Artery distributed throughout the head.
   ○ external carotid
   ○ external carrotid
   ○ externil carotid
   ○ external coratid

Arteries of the Body

As you work your way from the center down the body, you will see that the arteries divide into increasingly smaller and smaller branches. If you have ever seen figures or images of the arteries throughout the body, this is apparent. It becomes harder to distinguish individual arteries the smaller they get. For illustrative purposes we have provided this unlabeled figure of only the major arteries of the body. Smaller and more minor ones are not pictured at all.

As a medical transcriptionist, it will not be necessary for you to identify each and every artery pictured on this image (or the many more arteries too small to appear on this image). In an effort to make this portion of your training a little easier on the eyes and less cumbersome, arteries have been broken out by general body area, and several spelling exercises have been included. The important thing to notice is which body part you are studying. If necessary, refer back to this page and try to imagine the structures are relative to the figure above. For instance, when you study the arteries of the arm and hand, if it helps, look at that portion of this figure.

Artery names are made up of terms that you either already know or will know soon, such as *inferior thyroid, ascending cervical, pectoral branch, internal thoracic, dorsal of foot, lateral plantar, internal iliac, brachial, deep branch of the transverse cervical, pulmonary,* and *highest intercostal.*

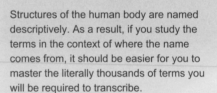

Structures of the human body are named descriptively. As a result, if you study the terms in the context of where the name comes from, it should be easier for you to master the literally thousands of terms you will be required to transcribe.

Before we list and explain the arteries, please direct your attention to a few descriptive terms that you will encounter in the names of the arteries and veins. The term *circumflex* means curved like a bow. Several arteries have this in their title: anterior humeral circumflex, scapular circumflex. *Princeps* is another term, and it means the principal or primary. It usually refers to the main artery of the structure named, such as princeps pollicis. The term *deep* is often used. This is just what it sounds like; it describes an artery or vein that is located deep or deeper within the body than a similarly named structure which is not deep. The word *profunda* (or profundus) also means deep. *Superficial* is the opposite of deep; it means that the structure is found close or closer to the surface of the body. Other terms are self-explanatory, such as *internal* and *external, highest,* or *branch.*

Finally, descriptive terms you learned earlier in this module are abundant in the naming of the arteries, such as *anterior, superior, medial,* and *lateral.* You should already know what these mean and it should be easy for you to apply the meanings to the arteries and veins.

The further into this module you get, the more you will be able to dissect the names given to the arteries—that is, break them down into their component parts. Instead of being overwhelmed by the sheer number of blood vessels in the human body (because it can certainly be staggering), you will see how the terms are built from the name and location of body structures. The important thing is to give you the tools you need to recognize, build, and understand the terms used in human anatomy and disease. If you can identify consistencies in the way that structures throughout the body are named, it will help you both to spell them and to be sure that you are correctly using them.

The fingers are called digits, and there are dorsal digital arteries, veins, nerves, and other anatomical structures. There is a pectoral muscle and likewise pectoral arteries and pectoral nerves. As you are introduced to the arteries, watch for the familiar modifying terms that describe the arteries as well: *inferior ulnar collateral arteries, inferior thyroid, superior pericardial*—the list goes on and on. If you are conscientious about learning the basic building blocks used to create the anatomical terms, there will be no need for you to memorize these thousands of words.

In the explanations of terms in the following pages, look for the names of additional arteries. For example, the term may be *interosseous*. The description will list several other arteries which also include this term as part of the name: *common interosseous artery, posterior interosseous artery, recurrent interosseous artery.* Instead of trying to memorize five or six different arteries, you only need to learn the word *interosseous* and from there can build (or more aptly—recognize) several different arteries.

Arteries of the Torso – Lesson 1

Following is a list of arteries found in the main part of the body, primarily the chest, abdominal, and pelvic regions. You will be exposed to some of the descriptive terms over and over throughout this anatomy module. Use the reiteration for review. Most of the terms listed are dictated with the word *artery* following, such as *splenic artery* or *bronchial arteries.*

   I. **TERMINOLOGY.**
      Enter each term in the space provided. Read the definition and description for each term.

      1. **aorta** _____

      The major systemic artery; this is the artery from which all others arise.

      2. **ascending aorta** _____

      Ascends from the left ventricle in the heart. The only branches off the ascending aorta are the right and left coronary arteries, which serve the myocardium (middle or muscle layer) of the heart.

      3. **aortic arch** _____

      After ascending and supplying the heart, the aorta arches posteriorly and to the left. This is known as the aortic arch.

      4. **innominate artery** _____

      Another name for the brachiocephalic artery.

      5. **brachiocephalic artery** _____

      The first branch of the aortic arch and one of the three vessels branching off the aortic arch.

      6. **left common carotid artery** _____

      Branches from the aorta and extends up the left side of the neck. Another one of the three vessels which branch off the aortic arch.

      7. **left subclavian artery** _____

      Extends from the aortic arch to the left side of the body. One of the three vessels which branch off the aortic arch.

8. **thoracic aorta** _____

A continuation of the aortic arch as it descends through the thoracic (chest) cavity to the diaphragm. It is a very large vessel and divides into major branches to the organs and muscles of the chest. Numerous branches supplying oxygen to the chest branch off the thoracic aorta.

9. **coronary** _____

Arteries that supply the heart.

10. **bronchial** _____

Provide circulation to the lungs.

II. **SPELLING.**
   Determine if the following words are spelled correctly. If the spelling is correct, leave the word as it has already been entered. If the spelling is incorrect, provide the correct spelling.

1. oarta _____   2. brochial _____

3. inominate _____   4. acending _____

5. subclavian _____

III. **MULTIPLE CHOICE.**
   Choose the correct term.

1. The major systemic artery.
   ◯ carotid
   ◯ aorta
   ◯ spermatic
   ◯ celiac

2. One of three vessels which comes off the aortic arch.
   ◯ inominate
   ◯ innominate
   ◯ enominate
   ◯ annominate

3. The arteries which enter the heart.
   ◯ coronary
   ◯ cornary
   ◯ coronory
   ◯ coranary

4. That part of the aorta which descends into the chest cavity.

◯ thoracic aorta

◯ thorasic aorta

◯ ascending aorta

◯ thoracec aorta

5. The first branch of the aortic arch.

◯ brachiacephalic artery

◯ brachicephalic artery

◯ brachiocephalec artery

◯ brachiocephalic artery

Arteries of the Torso – Lesson 2

I. TERMINOLOGY.
   Enter each term in the space provided. Read the definition and description for each term.

1. **esophageal** _____

Enters the esophagus as it passes through the mediastinum.

2. **cervical** _____

There are several cervical arteries: ascending cervical artery, deep cervical artery, descending cervical artery, superficial cervical artery, transverse cervical artery. These are in the cervical (neck) area.

3. **thyroid** _____

There is an inferior thyroid as well as an inferior thyroid artery of Cruveilhier, a lowest thyroid artery, and a superior thyroid artery. Finally, there is a thyrocervical trunk from which many arteries branch out.

4. **Cruveilhier** _____

An inferior thyroid artery.

5. **scapular** _____

There is a descending scapular artery, dorsal scapular artery, scapular circumflex artery, and transverse scapular artery. In addition to strictly scapular arteries, there are also the suprascapular and subscapular arteries. (Notice the use of *supra* and *sub* as prefixes.) These surround and/or supply the scapula.

6. **thoracic** _____

Include the highest thoracic arteries, internal thoracic arteries, and lateral thoracic arteries. In addition, there is a thoracoacromial artery and thoracodorsal artery. Notice that the last two are combined words. These are all found in the chest (thoracic) cavity.

7. **pulmonary** _____

There are both right and left pulmonary arteries which supply the right and left lungs. In fact, *pulmonary* means pertaining to the lung.

8. **coronary** _____

There are both right and left coronary arteries. These supply, respectively, the right atrium and ventricle and the left atrium and ventricle. *Coronary* actually means "encircling about like a crown." However, it is usually used in connection with the arteries, nerves, and other structures surrounding the heart.

9. **intercostal** _____

Supply the muscle between the ribs and structures of the chest wall. Intercostal means between the ribs.

10. **phrenic** _____

Supply blood to the diaphragm. There is a great phrenic artery as well as superior and inferior phrenic arteries. In addition, there is a musculophrenic artery and a pericardiophrenic artery.

II. SPELLING.
Determine if the following words are spelled correctly. If the spelling is correct, leave the word as it has already been entered. If the spelling is incorrect, provide the correct spelling.

1. esophagal _____   2. cervicle _____

3. intercostil _____   4. superficial _____

5. thoracodorsal _____

III. MULTIPLE CHOICE.
Choose the correct term.

1. The opposite of deep; found close or closer to the surface of the body.
   - ○ superficiall
   - ○ superfical
   - ○ supperficial
   - ○ superficial

2. A branch of the thyrocervical trunk.
   - ○ cruveilhier
   - ○ Cruveilhier
   - ○ Cruvielhier
   - ○ cruveihier

3. Means pertaining to the lung.

○ coronary
○ pulmonary
○ coranory
○ pulmanary

4. Artery supplying the area below the scapula.

○ subscapular
○ suboscapular
○ supscapular
○ subscapuler

5. Supplies blood to the diaphragm.

○ prenic
○ phrenic
○ frenic
○ phrenal

Arteries of the Torso – Lesson 3

I. **TERMINOLOGY.**
Enter each term in the space provided. Read the definition and description for each term.

1. **musculophrenic** _____

Arises from the internal thoracic artery and branches to lower part of pericardium.

2. **pericardiophrenic** _____

A long and slender branch of the internal thoracic artery. Relating to the pericardium and the diaphragm.

3. **abdominal aorta** _____

Also a very large vessel. It is specifically the segment of the aorta located between the diaphragm and the fourth lumbar vertebra.

4. **celiac** _____

This is the first branch of the abdominal aorta. It is a short, thick trunk which arises anteriorly just below the diaphragm. It immediately splits into three arterial branches (left gastric, hepatic, and splenic).

5. **splenic** _____

Goes into the spleen.

6. **left gastric** _____

Arises from the celiac artery and goes into the stomach.

7. **superior epigastric** _____

Arises from the internal thoracic artery, joins the inferior epigastric artery at the umbilicus, and supplies the anterior part of the abdominal wall and some of the diaphragm.

8. **gastroduodenal** _____

Small artery in the abdomen that supplies the stomach and duodenum.

9. **gastroepiploic** _____

Name of two different arteries (left and right gastro-omental) which supply the stomach and greater omentum.

10. **gastro-omental** _____

The left and right gastro-omental arteries branch from the splenic and gastroduodenal arteries, respectively, and supply the stomach and omentum.

II. **SPELLING.**
   Determine if the following words are spelled correctly. If the spelling is correct, leave the word as it has already been entered. If the spelling is incorrect, provide the correct spelling.

1. muculophrenic _____   2. hepatic _____

3. ommentum _____   4. carotid _____

5. sircumflex _____

III. **MULTIPLE CHOICE.**
   Choose the correct term.

1. Artery supplying the spleen.
   ◯ spleenic
   ◯ splenic
   ◯ splenia
   ◯ splenical

2. Means principal or primary.
   ◯ principle
   ◯ princeps
   ◯ princepis
   ◯ princips

3. An artery of the stomach.
   ◯ gastroeploic
   ◯ iliolumbar
   ◯ gastroepiploic
   ◯ gastrepiploic

4. An artery which is just a short, thick trunk.

○ seliac
○ ciliac
○ celiac
○ celliac

5. An artery of the pericardium and diaphragm.

○ percardiophrenic
○ spermatic artery
○ pericardophrenic
○ pericardiophrenic

Arteries of the Torso – Lesson 4

I. **TERMINOLOGY.**
Enter each term in the space provided. Read the definition and description for each term.

1. **hepatic** _____

Goes into the liver. There is both a common hepatic artery and a proper hepatic artery.

2. **mesenteric** _____

Both the superior and inferior mesenteric arteries arise from the abdominal aorta. They supply blood to the small intestine, cecum, appendix, ascending colon, transverse colon, large intestine, and rectum.

3. **renal** _____

Conduct blood to the kidneys.

4. **suprarenal** _____

Located just above the renal arteries and supply blood to the adrenal glands. There is an aortic suprarenal artery, inferior suprarenal artery, middle suprarenal artery, and superior suprarenal artery.

5. **cystic** _____

Distributes blood to the gallbladder (think cholecystectomy).

6. **pancreatic** _____

There are dorsal pancreatic, great pancreatic, and inferior pancreatic arteries.

7. **pancreaticoduodenal** _____

There are pancreaticoduodenal arteries, including a posterior superior pancreaticoduodenal, an anterior superior pancreaticoduodenal, and an inferior pancreaticoduodenal.

8. **colic** _____

There is a left colic artery, middle colic artery, right colic artery, right inferior colic artery, and superior accessory colic artery. These supply various sections of the colon, i.e. the ascending colon, transverse colon, descending colon.

9. **sigmoid** _____

Supply the sigmoid colon.

10. **appendicular** _____

Supplies the appendix.

II. SPELLING.
Determine if the following words are spelled correctly. If the spelling is correct, leave the word as it has already been entered. If the spelling is incorrect, provide the correct spelling.

1. hepatic _____   2. cystic _____

3. pancraetic _____   4. tranverse _____

5. suprarenal _____

III. MULTIPLE CHOICE.
Choose the correct term.

1. Means curved like a bow.
   ○ cercumflex
   ○ sircumflex
   ○ circumflex
   ○ circumflecks

2. Conducts blood to the kidneys.
   ○ renal artery
   ○ spermatic artery
   ○ rinal artery
   ○ kidney artery

3. Supplies the lower portion of the colon.
   ○ sigamoid
   ○ sigmiod
   ○ sigmoid
   ○ segmoid

4. Not one of the pancreatic arteries.

○ dorsal

○ inferior

○ ventral

○ great

5. Arteries which supply blood to many abdominal structures.

○ mezenteric

○ masseteric

○ mesenteric

○ mesanteric

Arteries of the Torso – Lesson 5

I. **TERMINOLOGY.**
   Enter each term in the space provided. Read the definition and description for each term.

1. **ileal** _____

Supply the ileum and are NOT to be confused with the iliac arteries, which are in a different part of the pelvis and supply the ilium (the hip bone).

2. **ileocolic** _____

There are also ileocolic arteries which supply various abdominal structures, arising from the lowest branch of the superior mesenteric artery.

3. **jejunal** _____

Supplies blood to the jejunum.

4. **spermatic** _____

Found only in males, these are a pair of small vessels which are just below the renal arteries and supply the gonads.

5. **ovarian** _____

Found only in females, they serve a similar function as above, except in women.

6. **vesical** _____

There are inferior and superior vesical arteries. These supply the bladder and ureters.

7. **common iliac** _____

Gives rise to both the internal and external iliac arteries and supplies the pelvis, abdominal wall, and lower legs.

8. **iliolumbar** _____

There is also an iliolumbar artery which branches off the internal iliac artery.

9. **middle sacral** _____

Arises from the very bottom of the abdominal aorta and supplies blood to the sacrum and coccyx.

10. **pudendal** _____

Both the internal and external pudendal arteries supply blood to the genitals, perineum, anus, and upper medial thigh.

II. **SPELLING.**
   Determine if the following words are spelled correctly. If the spelling is correct, leave the word as it has already been entered. If the spelling is incorrect, provide the correct spelling.

   1. ovarian _____   2. pedundal _____

   3. abdominal _____   4. internel _____

   5. external _____

III. **MULTIPLE CHOICE.**
   Choose the correct term.

   1. Found only in females.
      ◯ ovarian
      ◯ ovarien
      ◯ ovarion
      ◯ oviaron

   2. Supplies pelvis, abdominal wall, and lower legs.
      ◯ comon iliac
      ◯ common iliac
      ◯ common ileac
      ◯ uncommon iliac

   3. Supplies blood to the sacrum and coccyx.
      ◯ middle sacral
      ◯ middle coccal
      ◯ upper sacral
      ◯ lower sacral

4. Supply blood to the genitals, perineum, anus, and upper medial thigh.

○ pudendil
○ pughdendel
○ pudendal
○ pudendel

5. A pair of small vessels which are just below the renal arteries and supply the gonads.

○ spermatac
○ spermatic
○ spermatuc
○ spermitic

Arteries of the Arm – Lesson 1

By now you are surely beginning to see the high incidence of repetition in the naming of the arteries. There were only a few terms utilized in arterial nomenclature which you have not seen before. You will continue to see familiar terms throughout this unit and module. Again, notice the consistencies in spelling and terminology as you move through all the groups of arteries.

Following is a list of the arteries found in the arms. Pay close attention to spelling. Watch for familiar terms and try to identify possible surrounding structures such as muscles.

I. TERMINOLOGY.
   Enter each term in the space provided. Read the definition and description for each term.

   1. **axillary** _____

   The subclavian artery passes beneath the clavicle, carrying blood to the arm. It becomes the axillary artery as it passes underneath the armpit.

   2. **brachial** _____

   That same vessel becomes known as the brachial artery as it enters the upper arm region.

   3. **deltoid branch** _____

   There is also a deltoid branch which, of course, supplies the deltoid muscle.

   4. **humeral circumflex** _____

   There is both a posterior and anterior humeral circumflex artery wrapped around the humerus.

   5. **deep brachial** _____

   Both the deep brachial and superficial brachial arteries are branches of the brachial artery. They supply blood to the arm.

6. **ulnar collateral** _____

There are both superior and inferior ulnar collateral arteries. They are branches of the brachial artery. They supply blood to the triceps and elbow.

7. **medial collateral** _____

This is a branch of the deep brachial artery and also supplies the triceps muscle and elbow joint.

II. SPELLING.
Determine if the following words are spelled correctly. If the spelling is correct, leave the word as it has already been entered. If the spelling is incorrect, provide the correct spelling.

1. branchial* _____   2. colateral _____

3. humeral _____   4. axilary _____

5. ulner _____

*Branchial IS a medical term which means resembling the gills of a fish. It is not, however, appropriate in a discussion of arteries, the upper extremity, or in reference to "brachial," which is an unrelated word._

Arteries of the Arm – Lesson 2

I. TERMINOLOGY.
Enter each term in the space provided. Read the definition and description for each term.

1. **radial collateral** _____

Also a branch of the deep brachial artery, the radial collateral supplies the brachioradialis and brachialis muscles.

2. **ulnar recurrent** _____

There are both posterior and anterior branches of the ulnar recurrent artery. These supply the elbow joint region.

3. **radial recurrent** _____

A branch of the radial artery which supplies the brachioradialis, brachialis, and elbow region.

4. **interosseous** _____

There are several interosseous arteries, including the common interosseous, posterior interosseous, anterior interosseous, and recurrent interosseous. They distribute blood to various places within the arm. The word means "between bones."

5. **radial** _____

A fairly major artery off of the brachial artery. It supplies blood to the forearm, wrist, and hand.

6. **ulnar** _____

Also a fairly major artery off of the brachial artery, the ulnar artery distributes blood to the forearm, wrist, and hand.

7. **dorsal carpal branch of ulnar** _____

The name describes a specific branch of the ulnar artery. You already are familiar with _dorsal_ and _carpal_ so you should be able to ascertain where the blood supply goes.

II. SPELLING.
Determine if the following words are spelled correctly. If the spelling is correct, leave the word as it has already been entered. If the spelling is incorrect, provide the correct spelling.

1. radial _____   2. carple _____

3. recurent _____   4. interosseous _____

5. dorsil _____

Arteries of the Arm – Lesson 3

I. TERMINOLOGY.
Enter each term in the space provided. Read the definition and description for each term.

1. **superficial palmar branch of radial** _____

The name describes a specific branch of the radial artery. You are already familiar with _superficial_ and _palmar_ so you should be able to ascertain where the blood supply goes.

2. **palmar arch** _____

There are both deep and superficial palmar arches that supply the hand and specifically the palm.

3. **metacarpals** _____

There are both palmar and dorsal metacarpal arteries. These supply the metacarpals.

4. **common palmar digitals** _____

This artery and the following two arteries all supply the digits (fingers).

5. **proper palmar digitals** _____

Supplies the fingers.

6. **dorsal digitals** _____

Supplies the fingers.

7. **princeps pollicis** _____

The principal artery of the thumb.

8. **radialis indicis** _____

The radial artery of the index finger. It specifically supplies the index finger (first digit).

II. **SPELLING.**
   Determine if the following words are spelled correctly. If the spelling is correct, leave the word as it has already been entered. If the spelling is incorrect, provide the correct spelling.

   1. palmer _____   2. princeps _____

   3. metacarples _____   4. radialis _____

   5. policis _____

Arteries of the Leg – Lesson 1

A few new terms will be introduced in this unit. However, as before, there is also a great deal of repetition of the descriptive terms which you have already seen. Let's jump into arteries of the legs (pun intended!).

I. **TERMINOLOGY.**
   Enter each term in the space provided. Read the definition and description for each term.

   1. **common iliac arteries** _____

   The right and left common iliac arteries arise from the distal aorta in the posterior pelvic area. These pass down and divide into the internal and external iliac arteries.

   2. **internal iliac** _____

   Supplies the gluteal muscles and the organs of the pelvic region.

   3. **external iliac** _____

   Passes out of the pelvic cavity underneath the inguinal ligament. At this point it becomes the femoral artery.

   4. **femoral** _____

   The major artery from which several other vessels arise. It is derived from the word _femur_ for the femur bone in that area. There are several branches of the femoral artery which also are named for it: medial femoral circumflex, lateral femoral circumflex, common femoral, superficial femoral, deep femoral.

   5. **iliac circumflex** _____

   There is both a superficial and a deep iliac circumflex artery. These are near in proximity to the ilium bone.

   6. **gluteal** _____

   There are both superior and inferior gluteal arteries, which supply blood to the gluteal region.

7. **sacral** _____

There are both lateral and median sacral arteries. They supply the sacrum, coccyx, and rectum.

8. **pudendal** _____

There are both internal and external pudendal arteries. These were also covered in the arteries of the torso.

9. **obturator** _____

Arises off the internal iliac and supplies the pelvic muscles and hip joints.

10. **perforating** _____

There are three perforating arteries. These arise off the deep femoral artery and perforate (which means to pierce or bore through) the adductor magnus muscle to reach the back of the thigh. They supply the adductor, hamstring, gluteal muscles, and femur.

11. **genicular** _____

There are several genicular arteries, including the descending genicular, inferior lateral genicular, inferior medial genicular, middle genicular, superior lateral genicular, and superior medial genicular. The name is derived from the root word *genu* meaning "knee."

II. **SPELLING.**
Determine if the following words are spelled correctly. If the spelling is correct, leave the word as it has already been entered. If the spelling is incorrect, provide the correct spelling.

1. femeral _____   2. gluteal _____

3. sacril _____   4. ilieac _____

5. circumflex _____

III. MATCHING.
Match the term with the definition.

1. ____ femoral artery

2. ____ obturator artery

3. ____ iliac circumflex artery

4. ____ genicular artery

5. ____ gluteal artery

6. ____ common iliac arteries

7. ____ external iliac artery

8. ____ sacral artery

9. ____ pudendal artery

10. ____ internal iliac artery

A. near in proximity to the ilium bone

B. supplies gluteal muscles and organs of the pelvis

C. supplies sacrum, coccyx, and rectum

D. derived from the word 'femur,' for femur bone

E. supply blood to the gluteal region

F. passes out of pelvic cavity underneath inguinal ligament

G. supplies blood to external genitalia

H. arise from the distal aorta in the posterior pelvic area

I. supplies pelvic muscles and hip joints

J. name derived from root word 'genu' meaning knee

Arteries of the Leg – Lesson 2

I. TERMINOLOGY.
Enter each term in the space provided. Read the definition and description for each term.

1. **popliteal** _____

The femoral artery becomes the popliteal artery as it passes across the back of the knee. It is a large artery with several branches. It supplies the calf region.

2. **sural** _____

Arises off of the popliteal and supplies the calf region.

3. **tibial** _____

There are anterior and posterior tibial arteries, as well as anterior tibial recurrent. The name is derived from the tibia bone.

4. **fibular** _____

The fibular artery comes off the posterior tibial artery and has several branches, including a fibular circumflex branch. It supplies the ankle and deep calf muscles.

5. **peroneal** _____

The term peroneal literally means pertaining to the fibula or outer side of the leg. It is very important not to confuse this term with perineal, which is derived from perineum and refers to the region between the thighs. There is both a peroneal and a perforating peroneal artery. Quick tip: Remember the **o** in per**o**neal represents the **o**uter side of the leg.

6. **malleolar** _____

The term malleolus refers to a rounded protuberance. Usually when it is used in medical reports it is referring to the ankle. There is a medial malleolar branch, a lateral malleolar branch, a medial anterior malleolar artery, and a lateral anterior malleolar artery. They all basically supply the region of the ankle joint.

7. **dorsal of foot** _____

A continuation of the anterior tibial artery. It distributes blood to the foot and toes. The pulsation of blood through this artery is called the dorsalis pedis pulse and is often checked on examinations.

8. **dorsalis pedis pulse** _____

The pulsation of blood through the dorsal of foot.

9. **tarsal** _____

There are both a lateral tarsal artery and a medial tarsal artery. They distribute to the tarsus, which is the region between the foot and the leg.

10. **plantar** _____

There is a deep* plantar artery, an external plantar artery, a lateral plantar artery, and medial plantar artery. These supply the sole of the foot.

11. **arcuate** _____

Arises off the dorsal artery of the foot and supplies the foot and toes. The term arcuate means literally shaped like an arc and you may see this term used elsewhere.

12. **metatarsals** _____

There are both dorsal and plantar metatarsal arteries. Both of these descriptive terms should be familiar to you. These arteries distribute blood to the toes.

II. **SPELLING.**
   Determine if the following words are spelled correctly. If the spelling is correct, leave the word as it has already been entered. If the spelling is incorrect, provide the correct spelling.

1. popliteal _____   2. tibiel _____

3. maleolar _____   4. acruate _____

5. sureal _____

III. MULTIPLE CHOICE.
Choose the correct term.

1. This name is derived from the tibia bone.
   - ◯ popliteal
   - ◯ tarsal
   - ◯ tibial
   - ◯ plantar

2. Arises off the dorsal artery of the foot and supplies the foot and toes.
   - ◯ peroneal
   - ◯ arcuate
   - ◯ malleolar
   - ◯ tarsal

3. Arises off the popliteal and supplies the calf region.
   - ◯ metatarsals
   - ◯ tarsal
   - ◯ dorsal of foot
   - ◯ sural

4. Large artery with several branches which supplies the calf region.
   - ◯ popliteal
   - ◯ sural
   - ◯ metatarsals
   - ◯ tibial

5. Continuation of anterior tibial artery, it supplies blood to the foot and toes.
   - ◯ dorsalis pedis pulse
   - ◯ tibial
   - ◯ arcuate
   - ◯ dorsal of foot

6. Distributes to the tarsus.
   - ◯ sural
   - ◯ tarsal
   - ◯ arcuate
   - ◯ dorsal of foot

7. Pertaining to fibula or outer side of the leg.

   ○ perineal
   ○ popliteal
   ○ peroneal
   ○ plantar

8. Supplies the ankle and deep calf muscles.

   ○ fibular
   ○ dorsal of foot
   ○ metatarsals
   ○ arcuate

9. Supplies the sole of the foot.

   ○ popliteal
   ○ sural
   ○ plantar
   ○ metatarsis

10. Distribute blood to the toes.

    ○ malleolar
    ○ metatarsals
    ○ arcuate
    ○ plantar

Unit 6
Veins

Veins – Introduction

Having completed our studies of the arterial system by finishing up at the toes, we can now move forward to the other network of vessels in the body: veins. Even though there is a lot of information within the arteries and veins units of this module, just take it a piece at a time. Not every single blood vessel is listed. If you are not sure of a vein term that a dictator is using, check your medical dictionary. However, since you have learned most of the basic building blocks, the individual descriptive words in a name should be familiar.

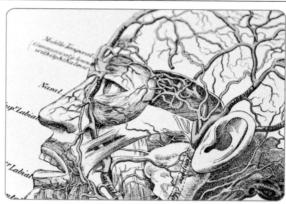

The blood flow through the arterial system is opposite to the blood flow in the venous system. Arteries give off smaller and smaller branches. In veins, the blood flows from smaller vessels into progressively larger ones. There are more veins than there are arteries—both deep and superficial. The superficial veins are the blue lines visible on most people, close to the surface of the skin (especially on the wrists). Some people's veins even protrude above the level of the skin. It is through these superficial veins that blood is drawn or intravenous injections are administered. The deep veins are close to the arteries and are generally similarly named.

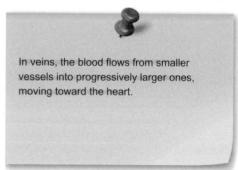

In veins, the blood flows from smaller vessels into progressively larger ones, moving toward the heart.

Blood flow of the veins is carried toward the heart. Eventually, all veins of the body converge into two major vessels which empty into the right atrium. These are the **superior vena cava** and the **inferior vena cava**. Again, all blood pumping back into the heart begins in small vessels and eventually converges into these two very large vessels.

Very closely related to the cardiovascular system, and to the veins in particular, is the lymphatic system. Its function is to transport fluid to the bloodstream, assist in fat absorption, and help protect the body from bacterial invasion. A fluid called **lymph** is composed of blood plasma minus certain macroproteins. It enters a network of lymph capillaries and is moved from there into larger lymph ducts, eventually also draining into the subclavian veins.

Lymph nodes are small, oval bodies composed of reticular tissue which is adapted specifically to filter lymph. They usually occur in clusters in specific regions of the body. **Germinal centers** within the node are the sites of lymphocyte production. The most common lymph nodes are the popliteal and **inguinal** (which means pertaining to the groin) nodes, the lumbar nodes (in the pelvic region), **cubital** and axillary nodes (the upper extremity), and the cervical nodes.

As mentioned previously, many veins have a corresponding or nearby artery with the same name. Therefore, this unit will be considerably shorter than the last. Just remember that the name of a vessel is not necessarily limited to only an artery or a vein, although occasionally this is the case.

FILL IN THE BLANK.
   Enter the term in the space provided.

1. superior vena cava_____

2. inferior vena cava_____

3. lymph_____

4. lymph nodes_____

5. germinal centers_____

6. inguinal_____

7. cubital_____

II. **MATCHING.**
   Match the term to the definition.

1. ____ Small, oval bodies, usually found in clusters.

2. ____ All veins eventually converge into two vessels. One of them is ____.

3. ____ Closely related to the cardiovascular system and especially the veins.

4. ____ Pertaining to the groin.

5. ____ The site of lymphocyte production.

A. superior vena cava
B. lymphatic system
C. lymph nodes
D. germinal centers
E. inguinal

Veins of the Head and Neck

The following figures are provided as a visual guide. The veins of the head and neck can be divided into three subdivisions.

1. The exterior head and facial veins
2. The neck veins
3. Veins of the brain and venous sinuses of dura mater (collectively called the diploic veins)

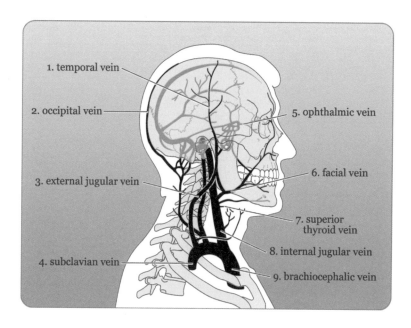

1. temporal vein
2. occipital vein
5. ophthalmic vein
3. external jugular vein
6. facial vein
7. superior thyroid vein
8. internal jugular vein
4. subclavian vein
9. brachiocephalic vein

I. FILL IN THE BLANK.
Label the veins of the head and neck in the corresponding boxes below.

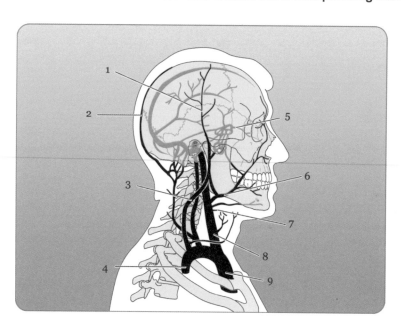

1. _____   2. _____

3. _____   4. _____

5. _____   6. _____

7. _____   8. _____

9. _____

II. SPELLING.
Determine if the following words are spelled correctly. If the spelling is correct, leave the word as it has already been entered. If the spelling is incorrect, provide the correct spelling.

1. jugular _____

2. opthalmic _____

3. brachycephalic _____

4. facial _____

5. ocipital _____

6. subclavien _____

7. temporal _____

8. thyriod _____

III. MULTIPLE CHOICE.
Determine which of the following is correctly spelled in each.

1. Two large veins that occur on each side of the neck.
   ◯ brachyocephalic
   ◯ brachiocephalic
   ◯ bracheocephalic
   ◯ brachieocephalic

2. Veins located in the orbital cavity.
   ◯ opthalmic
   ◯ ophthalamic
   ◯ ophthalmic
   ◯ opithalmic

3. Vein on the side of the head.
   ◯ temporal
   ◯ tempural
   ◯ tamporal
   ◯ tempural

4. Drains most of the blood from the face and scalp.
   ◯ external jugalar vein
   ◯ external jugular vein
   ◯ externil jugular vein
   ◯ externil gugular vein

5. Begins in a plexus at the back part of the skull.

○ ocipital vein
○ ocsipital vein
○ occiptal vein
○ occipital vein

6. Direct continuation of the angular vein.

○ facial vein
○ fascial vein
○ fashal vein
○ facial vain

7. Receives the superior laryngeal and cricothyroid veins.

○ superior thiroid vein
○ superior thryroid vein
○ superior thyroid vein
○ supierior thyroid vein

8. A continuation of the axillary vein.

○ subclevian vein
○ subclivian vein
○ subclavian vain
○ subclavian vein

Veins of the Body – Lesson 1

As you likely noticed, the veins of the head and neck are very similar to the arteries of the head and neck. Rather than continue through the rest of the body in the same manner that the arteries were introduced, we are going to cover the remainder of the veins of the body together in this unit. We will be skipping venous names you have already learned in the artery lessons, unless the vein is significant enough to the venous system to warrant additional description.

We will work our way down the body again, from top to bottom. A brief description of the vein will be included in the exercise below.

I. TERMINOLOGY.

Enter each term in the space provided. Read the definition and description for each term.

1. internal jugular _____

Extremely important to the venous system because all blood from the brain and deep areas of the face and neck are drained into it. There are two jugular veins, and they pass down the neck beside the common carotid arteries. They empty into the subclavian veins.

2. brachiocephalic _____

Also called innominate veins.

3. innominate _____

Where the subclavian and internal jugular veins come together. There are two of these, and they merge together to form the superior vena cava.

4. external jugular _____

The blood from the top of the head, part of the face, and the superficial neck region drain into these veins. They also empty into the subclavian veins.

5. diploic _____

There are several diploic veins, including the frontal diploic vein, occipital diploic vein, anterior temporal diploic vein, and posterior temporal diploic vein. These comprise the veins of the skull.

6. supratrochlear _____

These two veins begin high in the forehead and descend to the root of the nose.

7. retromandibular _____

Formed in the parotid gland by a union of the maxillary vein and the superficial temporal vein. It literally means behind the mandible.

II. SPELLING.

Determine if the following words are spelled correctly. If the spelling is correct, leave the word as it has already been entered. If the spelling is incorrect, provide the correct spelling.

1. inominate _____   2. brachiocephalic _____

3. juglar _____   4. supertrochlear _____

5. retromandiculer _____

III. MULTIPLE CHOICE.
Choose the best answer.

1. Veins of the skull.
   - ⭘ diploic
   - ⭘ diplioc
   - ⭘ diaploic
   - ⭘ dipolic

2. Major vein of the brain.
   - ⭘ internal jugular
   - ⭘ external jugular
   - ⭘ internal jugelar
   - ⭘ internal juguler

3. Veins which begin high in the forehead.
   - ⭘ supratroclear
   - ⭘ supertrochlear
   - ⭘ supratrachleor
   - ⭘ supratrochlear

4. Vein formed in the parotid gland.
   - ⭘ retromandiblar
   - ⭘ retormandibular
   - ⭘ retromandibular
   - ⭘ retromanbidular

5. Also referred to as innominate veins.
   - ⭘ brachycephalic
   - ⭘ brachyocephalic
   - ⭘ brachicephalic
   - ⭘ brachiocephalic

Veins of the Body – Lesson 2

I. TERMINOLOGY.
Enter each term in the space provided. Read the definition and description for each term.

1. **basilic** _____

A major superficial vein of the upper extremity. It passes on the ulnar side of the forearm and eventually forms the axillary vein.

2. **cephalic** _____

In addition to the cephalic vein, there are accessory cephalic and median cephalic veins. The cephalic vein is the other main superficial vein of the arm.

3. **median cubital** _____

A large branch of the cephalic vein which goes over the cubital fossa and joins with the basilic vein.

4. **median antebrachial** _____

Arises from the palmar venous plexus and passes up the forearm.

5. **plexus** _____

The term plexus means literally a network or tangle. It is a general term for a network of lymphatic vessels, nerves, or veins.

6. **azygos*** _____

In addition to the azygos vein, there is a left azygos and a lesser superior azygos vein. The azygos vein extends superiorly along the abdominal and thoracic walls on the right side of the vertebral column. At the level of T4 it joins directly with the superior vena cava.

7. **hemiazygos** _____

This is a tributary of the azygos vein.

8. **saphenous** _____

The small saphenous and the great saphenous veins are the superficial veins of the lower extremity. They are also called the greater saphenous and lesser saphenous veins. The greater saphenous is the longest vein of the body and is often harvested to repair vessels of the heart.

The term azygos spelled as such almost always refers to the azygos vein. However, there is a term azygous which means "having no fellow; unpaired." This term is often used as an adjective for other words. You should be aware of the difference.

II. SPELLING.

Determine if the following words are spelled correctly. If the spelling is correct, leave the word as it has already been entered. If the spelling is incorrect, provide the correct spelling.

1. cefalic _____

2. azygus _____

3. antibrachial _____

4. plexus _____

5. saphinous _____

III. MATCHING.

Match the term to the definition.

1. ____ A tributary of the azygos vein.

2. ____ A network or tangle.

3. ____ A main superficial vein in the arm.

4. ____ Superficial veins in the lower extremity.

5. ____ Main superficial vein in the arm which eventually forms the axillary vein.

A. hemiazygos

B. basilic

C. saphenous

D. plexus

E. cephalic

Unit 7
Bones

Bones – Introduction

The skeletal system is the basis of the human being's internal physical structure. The skeleton consists of the bones, and bones perform several important functions. First, the skeletal structure is the frame or the foundation of the body. It supports all other organs and tissues. Second, it protects the delicate vital organs. A good example of this is the skull, which encases the brain. Third, bones serve as levers for the muscles, the interaction of which makes breathing possible, as well as movement. Fourth, the marrow that is inside some bones produces blood cells. Finally, bones serve as calcium and phosphorus banks, which also provide bones with their rigidity and strength.

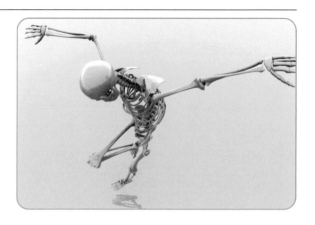

Don't worry—you aren't expected to memorize every single bone, muscle, artery, and microscopic vessel name within the human body! Of course, the more you know, the faster you'll be, and that means success as an MT. Remember, BenchMark KB carries many of Stedman's word books, which can be a huge resource for you! Have you logged in yet to check it out?

There are 206 bones in the human body. Bones are not inactive tissue. They contain a blood supply which allows for healing even severe breaks. They consist of protein fibers reinforced by calcium and phosphorus salts. Furthermore, as noted above, they contain bone marrow, which is where, among other things, red blood cells are produced.

The skeletal system is evaluated in the physical examination as part of what is called the musculoskeletal system. In fact, as far as practical medicine is concerned, bones are only able to be evaluated individually in x-ray examinations or surgeries. Thus, the terms related to bones are most common in orthopedics and radiology reports. However, that does not mean that they are exclusively used in these specialties.

Bones and Joints

Before we discuss the actual skeletal structure, you should become familiar with some common terms associated with bones. These terms are not specific bones (part of the 206), but rather have reference to parts of bones in general. It is not vital that you learn the definitions of the following terms, but you will type them as a transcriptionist. You should be confident in your ability to spell them and be aware that they are associated with the musculoskeletal system.

The bone itself is made up of several different parts. As mentioned, it is not *dead* tissue. Its dynamic nature makes it possible to heal fractures quickly. The following figure is of the femur bone. However, the parts of the bone that are labeled are common to almost all bones in the human skeleton.

1. epiphysis
2. metaphysis
4. periosteum
5. endosteum
3. diaphysis
2. metaphysis
1. epiphysis

The terms listed below deal with bones generally. Concentrate on spelling.

Terms	Definition
epiphysis	The expanded ends of a bone. (Plural is epiphyses.)
diaphysis	The main shaft of a long bone. (Plural is diaphyses.)
metaphysis	That part of the bone which is located between the epiphysis and the diaphysis.
periosteum	The connective tissue membrane which covers the bone.
endosteum	The thin membrane which lines the marrow cavity of a bone.

Two major types of tissue are associated with bones, although, as noted, there are obviously several different aspects to any given bone. These terms can be used to describe pathology specimens, radiological examinations, and operative reports that deal specifically with issues of the bones.

cortical bone	The adjectival form of the term cortex, which refers to the outer layer.
cancellous bone	A spongy structure, refers mostly to bone tissue.

There are three more terms commonly used in transcription that pertain to the bones themselves.

osteocytes	Mature bone cells.
lacunae	Small cavities containing mature bone cells. (Singular is lacuna.)
canaliculi	The narrow channels through which the osteocytes extend. (Singular is canaliculus.)

I. FILL IN THE BLANK.
Label the parts of the bone with the corresponding numbers.

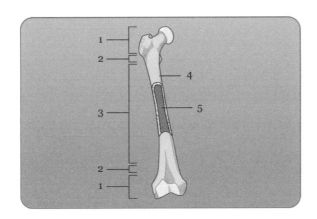

1. EPIPHYSIS

2. METAPHYSIS

3. DIAPHYSIS

4. PERIOSTEUM

5. ENDOSTEUM

II. SPELLING.

Determine if the following words are spelled correctly. If the spelling is correct, leave the word as it has already been entered. If the spelling is incorrect, provide the correct spelling.

1. epiphysis ✓
2. cortical ✓
3. periostum PERIOSTEUM
4. lacunae ✓
5. cannaliculi CANALICULI
6. metaphysis ✓
7. ostecytes OSTEOCYTES
8. endosteum ✓
9. diaphisis DIAPHYSIS
10. cancelous CANCELLOUS

III. MULTIPLE CHOICE.
Select the appropriate answer.

1. (⊗Lacunae, ◯ Lacuna, ◯ Laccunae) are small cavities of mature bone cells.

2. Bone tissue which is spongy is (◯cancelous, ◯ cancellus, ⊗ cancellous) bone.

3. The (⊗diaphysis, ◯ diaphyses, ◯ diphysis) is the main shaft of a long bone.

4. (◯Endosium, ⊗ Endosteum, ◯ Endostum) is the lining of the marrow cavity.

5. The outer layer of a bone is called the (◯corticle, ◯ cortikal, ⊗ cortical) bone.

6. The (◯metaphisis, ◯ metaphyses, ⊗ metaphysis) is between the epiphysis and the diaphysis.

7. (⊗Canaliculi, ◯ Cannaliculi, ◯ Canaliculie) are narrow channels of osteocytes.

8. (◯Epiphyses, ◯ Epiphisis, ⊗ Epiphysis) refers to the expanded end of a bone.

9. The membrane surrounding the bone is called the (◯perosteum, ⊗ periosteum, ◯ peryosteum).

10. (◯Ostecytes, ⊗ Osteocytes, ◯ Osteocyts) are mature bone cells.

Axial Skeleton

The bones of the human skeleton are placed into two divisions: the axial skeleton and the appendicular skeleton.

Axial skeleton: The axial skeleton has 80 bones, and includes the bones of the skull, vertebral column, thoracic cage, sternum, hyoid, and ears.

- Skull 21 (8 paired and 5 unpaired)
- Ossicles of Ears 6 (3 per side)
- Lower Jaw 1
- Hyoid Bone 1
- Vertebrae 26 bones
- Chest 25 bones
- Total 80

Following is a list of the bones in the axial skeleton.

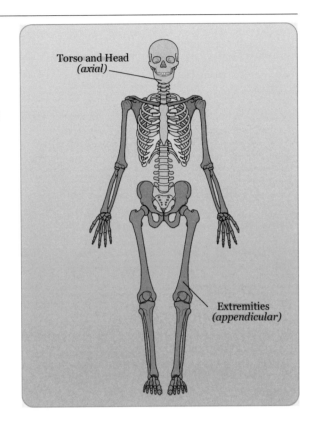

I. **FILL IN THE BLANK.**
   Enter the term listed in the space provided. Do not include the numbers in parentheses next to the terms.

   Spelling is the key factor. Make sure that you spell each term correctly so that you can begin to recognize the correct spelling. After you enter the word, review the part of the body each bone belongs to (see header above each list).

   SKULL (8 paired bones for a total of 16)

   1. inferior nasal concha_____

   2. lacrimal_____

   3. maxilla_____

   4. nasal_____

   5. palatine_____

   6. parietal_____

   7. temporal_____

   8. zygomatic_____

SKULL (5 unpaired for a total of 5)

   9. ethmoid_____

  10. frontal_____

  11. occipital_____

  12. sphenoid_____

  13. vomer_____

OSSICLES OF EACH EAR (3 per side for a total of 6)

  14. incus_____

  15. malleus_____

  16. stapes_____

LOWER JAW (1 for a total of 1)

  17. mandible_____

HYOID BONE (1 for a total of 1)

  18. hyoid_____

VERTEBRAL COLUMN (26 total bones, differentiated below)

  19. cervical vertebrae (7)_____

  20. atlas (1st cervical vertebra)_____

  21. axis (2nd cervical vertebra)_____

  22. thoracic vertebrae (12)_____

  23. lumbar vertebrae (5)_____

  24. sacrum_____

  25. coccyx_____

CHEST (25 total)

  26. sternum_____

  27. ribs (12 pairs)_____

Axial Skeleton – Skull (Part A)

The axial skeletal system consists of, as previously noted, the bones of the skull, vertebral column, thoracic cage, sternum, hyoid, and ears. This creates the structure for most of the vital areas of the body, providing support and protection for the inner organs, as well as movement through the neck and the spine.

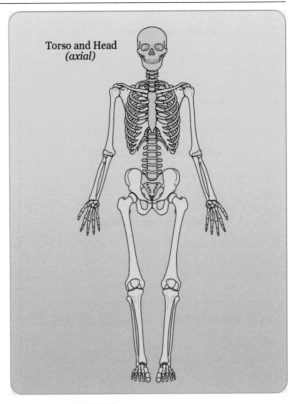

Torso and Head
(axial)

Bones of the Skull

There are 29 bones in the skull. The cranium contains 8 bones, the face has 15 bones, and the ossicles of the ears have 6 bones (3 per ear).

Fontanels

At birth, the bones of the head are not completely formed. As a result, there is adequate space between them to allow the baby's head to be molded enough to fit through the birth canal. These 6 spaces are known as **fontanels** or soft spots.

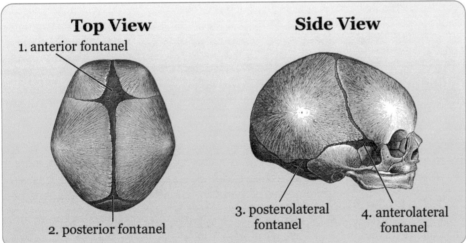

Top View
1. anterior fontanel
2. posterior fontanel

Side View
3. posterolateral fontanel
4. anterolateral fontanel

After birth, the bones of the cranium continue to grow until the fontanels are no longer present. The posterior and anterolateral fontanels usually fill in 2–3 months after birth. The posterolateral fontanels usually fill in at the end of the first year. The anterior fontanel (the largest fontanel) usually fills in by the middle of the second year after birth.

I. TERMINOLOGY.
Enter each term in the space provided. Read the definition and description for each term.

1. **anterior fontanel** _____

The space where the frontal angles of the parietal bones meet the two ununited halves of the frontal bone.

2. **posterior fontanel** _____

The space where the occipital angles of the parietal bones meet the occipital.

3. **anterolateral fontanels** _____

An interval on either side of the head where the frontal angle of the temporal bone and greater wing of the sphenoid meet. (2)

4. **posterolateral fontanels** _____

The interval on either side of the head between the mastoid angle of the parietal bone, the temporal bone, and the occipital bone. (2)

Axial Skeleton – Skull (Part B)

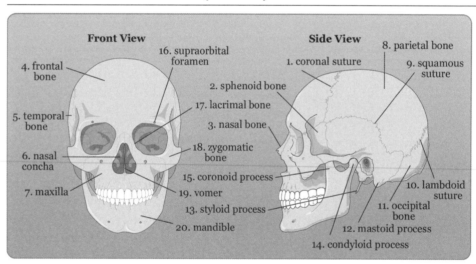

Sometimes it helps to be able to visualize a body part in order to associate the proper terms with body placement. This figure shows exactly where the structures listed appear in the body. Not all structures can be seen in the angles demonstrated. (For example, the palatine bone is in the roof of the mouth, which cannot be visualized on the figure below.) Remember, it is not necessary to memorize every figure in this unit. However, if it helps for you to visualize, the following figures will make that easier.

In addition to the terms you see listed, additional terms may appear on figures. All of the terms that appear in these figures were chosen because of their occurrence in medical transcription. If you transcribe the types of reports that deal with these parts of the body, you will see these terms often.

Our emphasis in Anatomy and Disease is on spelling and a general familiarity with these terms.

I. FILL IN THE BLANK.
Label the parts of the skull in the corresponding boxes.

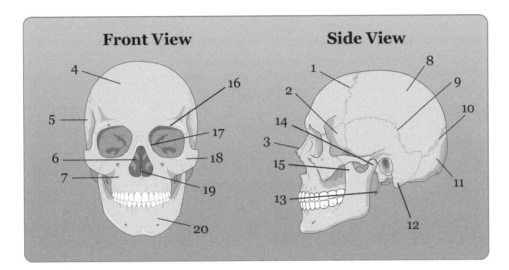

1. CORONAL SUTURE

2. SPHENOID BONE

3. NASAL BONE

4. FRONTAL BONE

5. TEMPORAL BONE

6. NASAL CONCHA

7. MAXILLA

8. PARIETAL BONE

9. SQUAMOUS SUTURE

10. LAMBDOID SUTURE

11. OCCIPITAL BONE

12. MASTOID PROCESS

13. STYLOID PROCESS

14. CONDYLOID PROCESS

15. CORONOID PROCESS

16. SUPRAORBITAL FORAMEN

17. LACRIMAL BONE

18. ZYGOMATIC BONE

19. VOMER

20. MANDIBLE

II. SPELLING.
Determine if the following words are spelled correctly. If the spelling is correct, leave the word as it has already been entered. If the spelling is incorrect, provide the correct spelling.

1. ethmoid ✓

2. choronal CORONAL

3. sphenoid ✓

4. concha ✓

5. vomir VOMER

6. mandible ✓

7. foramen ___✓___   8. superorbital _SUPERORBITAL_

9. ocipital _OCCIPITAL_   10. squamus _SQUAMOUS_

11. nazal _NASAL_   12. maxilla ___✓___

13. lacrimel _LACRIMAL_   14. zygomatic ___✓___

15. pariatel _PARIETAL_   16. temperal _TEMPORAL_

17. condoloid _CONDYLOID_   18. frontal ___✓___

19. lamdoid _LAMBDOID_   20. coronoid ___✓___

III. MULTIPLE CHOICE.
Choose the term which has the correct spelling.

1. The ((⊗)ethmoid, ◯etmoid, ◯ethymoid) is part of the skull and literally means "sieve-like."

2. The occiput gives rise to the (◯ocipital, ⊗ occipital, ◯ occipitle) bone and is the posterior part of the head.

3. The term (◯nazal, ◯ nasle, ⊗ nasal) denotes relationship to the nose.

4. (⊗Concha, ◯Concae, ◯Conchae) means literally "a shell" and is used to describe structures which are shell-like in shape.

5. The (◯mandibal, ⊗ mandible, ◯ mandable) is the lower jaw bone.

6. (⊗Zygomatic, ◯Zigomatic, ◯Zycomatic) can describe either a process, a bone, or an arch.

7. A (◯foramin, ◯forramen, ⊗foramen) is a natural opening or passage.

8. The upper jaw is made up of the (◯maxila, ⊗maxilla, ◯macksilla).

9. Shaped like a Greek letter is the (⊗lambdoid, ◯lamdoid, ◯lamboid) suture.

10. (◯Condaloid, ⊗Condyloid, ◯Chondyloid) means resembling a knuckle or rounded bone.

Axial Skeleton – Vertebral Column

The vertebral column is a major support structure for the human body. It consists of 26 bones that are all superimposed on one another, but separated by intervertebral discs. A designated space for passage of the spinal cord runs through the vertebral column housing the core of the central nervous system. In other words, the spinal cord runs right through the center of the bony vertebral column, protecting it from injury.

The vertebral column is not straight like a stack of checkers. The spine has a curvature with portions being convex (rounded like the outside of a sphere) and others being concave (rounded, depressed like the hollowed inner surface of a sphere).

- cervical vertebrae (7)
- atlas vertebra (the first cervical vertebra)
- axis vertebra (the second cervical vertebra)
- thoracic vertebrae (12)
- lumbar vertebrae (5)
- sacrum
- coccyx

Term	Description	Notes
cervical spine	7 vertebrae located in the neck area	Abbreviated C1–C7; concave
thoracic spine	12 vertebrae located in the upper back	Abbreviated T1–T12; convex
lumbar spine	5 vertebrae located in the lower back	Abbreviated L1–L5; concave
sacral spine	5 fused sacral vertebrae	Two sides are smooth for joining with pelvic bones; resembles a triangle
coccyx	Single bone fused from 4–5 coccygeal vertebrae at base of spine	Also called the tailbone
articulate	Articulate means to loosely connect or join	Thoracic vertebrae articulate to 12 ribs to create a protective cavity for the heart and lungs (thoracic cavity)
intervertebral discs	Fibrous tissue and cartilage between the vertebrae to absorb spinal compression and shock	Disc also correctly spelled disk

In radiology, as well as other specialties in which the spine is referred to, the name of the spine will be abbreviated with its beginning letter. The cervical spine becomes the C-spine, the thoracic spine the T-spine, and the lumbar spine the L-spine (or LS for lumbosacral). If a dictator is referring to an individual vertebra within a given spine, or a level of the spine, he will attach the number to the abbreviated spine that he is talking about. For example, he may dictate, "There is spondylolisthesis of C5 on C6," or, "The C7-T1 level is normal."

You should be able to recognize and understand what a dictator is referring to when he says such letters and numbers. (When we say "he," we certainly realize this could also be "she.") As a transcriptionist, it is correct to delineate the spines and spine levels as illustrated below.

These terms represent the structures of the spine. The spinal column is part of the axial skeleton.

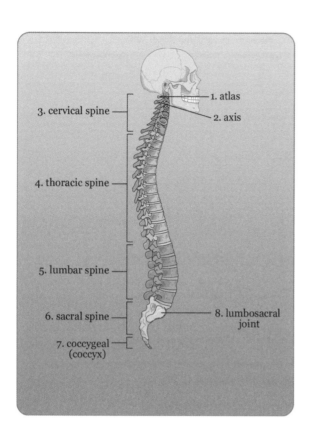

I. **FILL IN THE BLANK.**
   Label the vertebral column by entering the term into the corresponding box below. Be sure to spell correctly.

1. ATLAS

2. AXIS

3. CERVICAL SPINE

4. THORACIC SPINE

5. LUMBAR SPINE

6. SACRAL SPINE

7. COCCYGEAL (COCCYX)

8. LUMBOSACRAL JOINT

II. MATCHING.
Match the correct term to the definition.

1. _G_   lumbar spine
2. _F_   intervertebral discs
3. _B_   cervical spine
4. _E_   thoracic spine
5. _D_   articulate
6. _A_   sacral spine
7. _C_   coccyx

A.   triangular shaped
B.   the neck
C.   tailbone
D.   join
E.   connects to the ribs
F.   between the bones of the spine
G.   lower back

III. FILL IN THE BLANK.
Use the word(s) in the box to fill in the blanks.

1. Consisting of five vertebrae, the _LUMBAR SPINE_ is the lower back.

2. _ARTICULATE_ means loosely connect.

3. Consisting of seven vertebrae, the _CERVICAL SPINE_ makes up the bones of the neck.

4. Five fused vertebrae make up the _SACRAL SPINE_.

5. The _THORACIC SPINE_ corresponds to the chest cavity and consists of 12 vertebrae.

6. The _COCCYX_ is also called the tailbone.

7. The spine is made up of several discs; the cartilage and fibrous tissue between them are called _INTERVERTEBRAL DISCS_

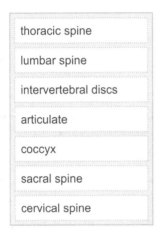

| thoracic spine |
| lumbar spine |
| intervertebral discs |
| articulate |
| coccyx |
| sacral spine |
| cervical spine |

Appendicular Skeleton

All of the terms found in the previous figures are part of the *axial skeleton*. The second type of skeleton is the *appendicular skeleton*. Following is an illustration of the appendicular skeleton. (It should be noted that the cervical vertebrae, sternum, and ribs are part of the axial skeleton, even though they appear on the appendicular skeleton figure.)

You may find it helpful to review terminology like *anterior*, *distal*, *lateral*, *inferior*, *posterior*, *superior*, and *medial*, as these terms are often used in anatomy for orientation.

Unlike most of the figures that you see in this unit, "The Human Skeleton" is one that you should memorize. These are the basic supportive structures of the body and, as such, are terms that you will commonly see throughout medical transcription. In addition, there are instances in which a knowledge of not only the spelling but also the body placement of these terms will be important.

You will need to differentiate between the carpals/ metacarpals (the bones of the hands and wrist) and the tarsals/metatarsals (bones of the ankles and feet). For some reason, there are dictators who have not quite picked this up. You may notice while transcribing an x-ray report of the upper extremities (the arms) that the dictator refers to the *metatarsals* or the *tarsals*. There are no tarsals of any kind in the arms!

Also, the hands are in no way connected to the feet. This seems obvious to a lay person. However, as mentioned, it is not uncommon for a dictator to confuse the terms *carpals* and *tarsals*. Sometimes a dictator will even create an articulation of these bones which is anatomically impossible, such as the carpometatarsal joint. Visualize this for a moment. That would make a very strange-looking person.

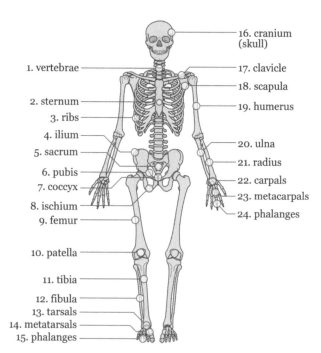

Ilium is another term that is found on the appendicular skeleton and is easy to confuse. This is a bone of the hip and is spelled I-L-I-U-M. There is an organ of the gastrointestinal system which is called the ileum and is spelled I-L-E-U-M. If you know that I-um is in the hip and E-um is next to the stomach, it can save you the embarrassment of silly mistakes or precious time spent looking in a medical dictionary.

In addition to the now-familiar bones of the axial skeleton, the human skeleton has appendicular bones of many shapes and sizes. Take a few minutes to study the bones of the appendicular skeleton.

The appendicular skeleton consists of:

- clavicle (collarbone) (1 per side for a total of 2)
- scapula (shoulder blade) (1 per side for a total of 2)
- arm bones (3 per side for a total of 6)
    - humerus (upper arm)
    - radius (forearm)
    - ulna (forearm)

- carpal (wrist) (8 per side for a total of 16)
- metacarpal (hand) (5 per side for a total of 10)
- phalanges (fingers) (14 per side for a total of 28)
- os coxae (hip/pelvic bone) (1 per side for a total of 2)
- femur (thigh) (1 per side for a total of 2)
- patella (kneecap) (1 per side for a total of 2)
- tibia (leg) (1 per side for a total of 2)
- fibula (leg) (1 per side for a total of 2)
- tarsal (ankle) (7 per side for a total of 14)
- metatarsal (foot) (5 per side for a total of 10
- phalanges (toes) (14 per side for a total of 28)

Memorize the human skeleton and do the accompanying exercises.

I. **FILL IN THE BLANK.**
   Label the skeleton by entering the term in the corresponding box.

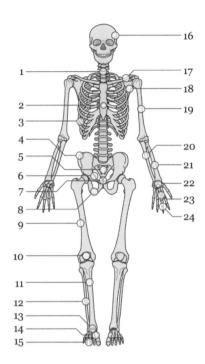

1. VERTEBRAE

2. STERNUM

3. RIBS

4. ILIUM

5. SACRUM

6. PUBIS

7. COCCYX

8. ISCHIUM

9. FEMUR

10. PATELLA

11. TIBIA

12. FIBULA

13. TARSALS

14. METATARSALS

15. PHALANGES

16. CRANIUM (SKULL)

17. CLAVICLE

18. SCAPULA

19. HUMERUS

20. ULNA

21. RADIUS

22. CARPALS

23. METACARPALS

24. PHALANGES

II. FILL IN THE BLANK.
Enter the correct word in the blank provided.

1. The bone which runs between the two sets of ribs is the _STERNUM_ .

2. There are five sets of bones which make up the pelvis. They are the pubis, _ILIUM_ ,
    3. _SACRUM_ , 4. _COCCYX_ and the ischium.

5. There are three sets of bones which make up the ankles/feet. They are the _TARSALS_ ,
    6. _METATARSALS_ , and 7. _PHALANGES_ .

8. Four bones make up the leg; they are the femur, _PATELLA_ , tibia, and the
    9. _FIBULA_ .

10. The shoulder consists of the _CLAVICLE_ and the 11. _SCAPULA_ .

12. The bones which hold up the head are the _VERTEBRAE_ .

13. The sternum divides the _RIBS_ .

14. The main bone of the upper arm is the _HUMERUS_ .

15. The two bones of the forearm are the _ULNA_ and the radius.

16. The name of the head bone is the _CRANIUM_ or 17. _SKULL_ .

18. The bones of the wrist and hand are the _CARPALS_ , 19. _METACARPALS_ , and
    20. _PHALANGES_ .

Appendicular Skeleton – Diagram

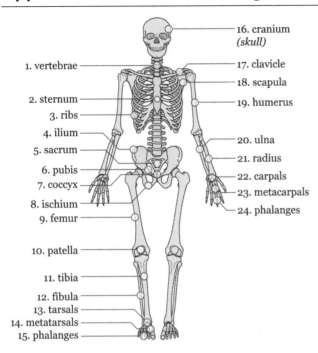

1. vertebrae
2. sternum
3. ribs
4. ilium
5. sacrum
6. pubis
7. coccyx
8. ischium
9. femur
10. patella
11. tibia
12. fibula
13. tarsals
14. metatarsals
15. phalanges
16. cranium (skull)
17. clavicle
18. scapula
19. humerus
20. ulna
21. radius
22. carpals
23. metacarpals
24. phalanges

I. SPELLING.

Determine if the following words are spelled correctly. If the spelling is correct, leave the word as it has already been entered. If the spelling is incorrect, provide the correct spelling.

1. pubis _____ ✓ _____
2. radious _____ RADIUS _____
3. carples _____ CARPALS _____
4. patela _____ PATELLA _____
5. ishium _____ ISCHIUM _____
6. ilium _____ ✓ _____
7. coccyx _____ ✓ _____
8. tarsels _____ TARSALS _____
9. vertebray _____ VERTEBRAE _____
10. clavicle _____ ✓ _____

Appendicular Skeleton – Shoulder Bones

The shoulder consists of three bones: the clavicle, scapula, and humerus. The joints of the shoulder are the articulations between shoulder bones.

The clavicle (or collarbone) is shaped like a loose S and allows the arm to move freely by holding the corresponding shoulder away from the chest. It is the first bone of the human body to ossify. The clavicle is comprised of cancellous bone covered by cortical bone with no bone marrow. The medial or sternal end is attached to the sternum, and the lateral or acromial end is attached to the acromion of the scapula.

The scapula or shoulder blade is positioned over ribs 2–7 and lies against

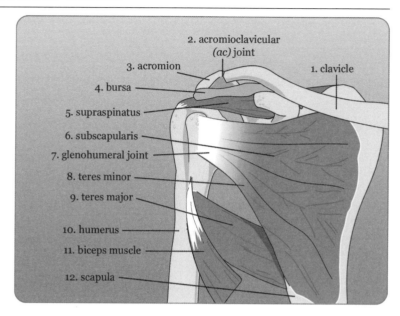

the posterior aspect of the ribcage. There are several prominent parts of the scapula: the spine, a long bone that extends to the acromion to form the point of the shoulder; the coracoid; and the glenoid cavity, where the head of the humerus rests.

The humerus is the upper arm bone. It is a long bone with two ends. The superior end, or the head, is the rounded end and connects to the glenoid cavity of the scapula to form the shoulder joint. This is a ball and socket joint. Below the head is the anatomical neck which has a small groove/indentation located just beneath the head. Below the anatomical neck is the surgical neck, then the long shaft of the humerus, and finally the inferior end of the bone. The inferior end has lateral and medial epicondyles that are insertion points for muscles of the forearm. An easy way to distinguish the humerus from the femur is to remember that it is not very humorous to hit your funny bone (which presses on a nerve near the elbow, causing intense pain).

I. **TRUE/FALSE.**
   The following are spelled correctly: true or false?

   1. humerous

      ◯ true

      ⊘ false

   2. scapula

      ⊗ true

      ◯ false

   3. clavicle

      ⊗ true

      ◯ false

4. glenoide cavity

   ◯ true
   ⊗ false

5. acromiel end

   ◯ true
   ⊗ false

II. **MULTIPLE CHOICE.**
   Choose the best answer.

   1. The humerus is a _____.

      ⊗ long bone
      ◯ short bone
      ◯ wormian bone
      ◯ irregular bone

   2. The clavicle is shaped like the letter _____.

      ◯ A
      ◯ N
      ⊗ S
      ◯ X

   3. The upper arm bone is called the _____.

      ⊗ humerus
      ◯ femur
      ◯ scapula
      ◯ calvicle

   4. Which of the following is NOT related to the scapula?

      ◯ glenoid cavity
      ◯ acromion
      ⊗ epicondyle
      ◯ coracoid

   5. Which bone lies against the rib cage, between ribs 2 and 7?

      ◯ clavicle
      ⊗ scapula
      ◯ humerus
      ◯ acromion

Appendicular Skeleton – Arm Bones

The forearm is composed of two separate bones:

- radius
- ulna

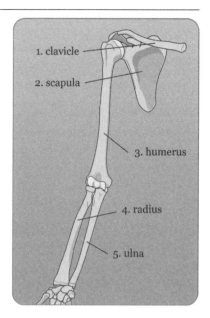

1. clavicle
2. scapula
3. humerus
4. radius
5. ulna

The **radius** is one of two bones of the forearm. It is located on the thumb side of the forearm. It has a flattened head at the superior portion where it articulates with the humerus. Further down, below the neck, is a tuberosity or prominence that is the insertion site for the tendons of the biceps. At the inferior end lies the styloid process for articulation to the carpals. It forms a margin for the tendons of two muscles to the thumb.

The **ulna** is the other bone of the forearm and is located on the little finger side. The proximal end of the ulna connects to the elbow to form the elbow joint. Although the radius also articulates with the elbow, the ulna has a stronger connection. Other parts of the ulna include the olecranon, which forms the point of the elbow; the trochlear notch; the coronoid process; the radial notch, where the ulna and radius articulate; the head, which articulates with the wrist and hand; and the styloid process, a bony prominence that can be palpated on the ulnar aspect of the wrist when the hand is palm down.

Human wrists, hands, and fingers have incredible dexterity and range of motion. The fine motor ability of the human hand is due in large part to the framework of bones with their many muscle and tendon attachments.

- carpals
- metacarpals
- phalanges

The **carpals** are the wrist bones. They articulate with the ulna. Carpals are generally made up of 2 rows of 4 bones each and are held in place by ligaments. The 8 carpal bones are the hamate, scaphoid, trapezium, pisiform, trapezoid, lunate, triquetrum, and capitate bones.

The **metacarpal** bones are the bones of the hands. They consist of 5 bones that form the structure of the hand and articulate with the carpals. These metacarpals are numbered from 1–5, with the thumb being first and the little finger fifth.

The **phalanges** articulate with the metacarpals to form the fingers. There are 5 fingers, and each has 3 phalanges (the distal, medial, and proximal phalanges) with the exception of the thumb, which has only 2.

Take a few minutes to feel the olecranon by bending your elbow and using your fingers to find the point. Then, putting your palm down, run your fingers along the ulnar (outer) aspect of your wrist. Do you feel the styloid process? Study the graphic and closely examine the radius and ulna. Do you see where the ulnar and radius articulate (join) at the radial notch? Can you identify the head where the radius articulates with the wrist and hand? Finally, think about the definition of trochlea (pulley or structure resembling a pulley) as you flex and extend your elbow. In addition to the elbow (trochlear notch), where else might your body have pulley-shaped parts or structures? There is a fibrocartilaginous pulley in the frontal bone through which passes the tendon that controls the movement of the superior oblique eye muscle known as the trochlea musculi obliqui, superioris oculi. You used an ocular pulley system to read this!

I. FILL IN THE BLANK.
Enter the term in the space provided (8 carpal bones).

1. hamate_____

2. scaphoid_____

3. trapezium_____

4. pisiform_____

5. trapezoid_____

6. lunate_____

7. triquetrum_____

8. capitate_____

II. MATCHING.
Match the term to the definition.

1. _G_ phalanges

2. _C_ ulna

3. _D_ carpals

4. _H_ tuberosity

5. _A_ metacarpals

6. _E_ olecranon

7. _F_ radial notch

8. _B_ radius

A. hands
B. thumb-side bone
C. pinky-side bone
D. wrists
E. point of elbow
F. joint of the ulna and radius
G. fingers
H. prominence

III. MULTIPLE CHOICE.
Choose the best answer.

1. The forearm bone closest to the pinky.
   ⊗ ulna
   ◯ radius

2. The forearm bone closest to the thumb.
   ◯ ulna
   ⊗ radius

3. Which of the following is not part of the ulna?
   ◯ coronoid process
   ◯ olecranon
   ⊗ malleolus
   ◯ styloid process

4. A bony prominence.

   ○ olecranon
   ⊗ tuberosity
   ○ radial notch

5. Allows articulation with the carpals.

   ○ olecranon
   ⊗ styloid process

Appendicular Skeleton – Hip and Upper Leg

Two of the bones of the lower extremities consist of the os coxae and the femur.

- os coxae
- femur

Os coxae

The hip bone is also called the os coxae. If you view the pelvic girdle anteriorly, it resembles the mask of a superhero. It looks like a hat with wings sitting on top of a mask to cover the eyes. The wings form the ilium, the top of which is the iliac crest. The part of the mask that goes over the eyebrows is formed by the pubic bones. The lower part of the eye mask is formed by the ischium bones, and the portion between the eyes is the symphysis pubis. This lies on the pubic arch. Just think of a superhero when trying to remember the bones of the pelvis. Also remember that *Ilium* is the hip bone and *ileum* is gastric related. Just think of the letter *e* having a loop, like a loop of bowel. This will save you precious time in your studies and on the job in order to distinguish these two.

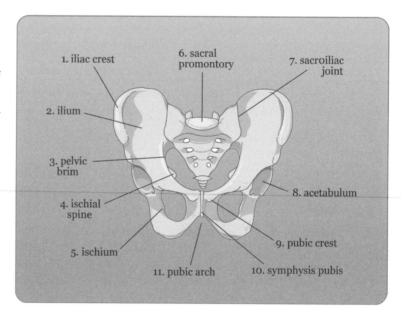

1. iliac crest
6. sacral promontory
7. sacroiliac joint
2. ilium
3. pelvic brim
4. ischial spine
5. ischium
8. acetabulum
9. pubic crest
11. pubic arch
10. symphysis pubis

To support childbearing, the female pelvis is larger than the male pelvis. Unlike the male pelvic structure, the female pelvis has a wide subpubic arch and a forward tilt; the ischial bones are turned outwards and the symphysis pubis is shallow. In addition, the bones of the female pelvis are thin.

Femur

The femur (or thigh bone) is the longest and strongest bone in the body. It articulates with the pelvis and two smaller leg bones to form the thigh. At its most superior point the femur consists of a head, neck, greater trochanter, and lesser trochanter. The head of the femur is knob-like and fits perfectly into the acetabulum of the os coxae (to form a ball and socket joint). The greater and lesser trochanters are bony prominences where muscles attach.

The long middle section of the femur is a rounded shaft. At the most inferior end of the shaft are two protrusions (to which ligaments and tendons attach) called the medial epicondyle and the lateral epicondyle. Situated between these two epicondyles is the patellar surface, where the patella or kneecap connects.

A good way to visualize the femur is to think of it as an old-fashioned Barbie doll leg. When Barbie's leg would come off, you had to pop the head of the femur back into the hip (ahh, the good old days!).

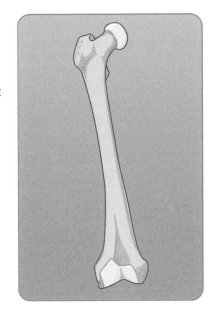

I. MATCHING.
Match the correct term to the definition.

1. _B_ femur
2. _D_ ischium
3. _C_ acetabulum
4. _E_ os coxae
5. _A_ patella

A. kneecap
B. thigh bone
C. the head of the femur fits into this
D. lower part of the "eye mask"
E. hip bone

II. MULTIPLE CHOICE.
Choose the best answer.

1. The superior portion of the femur consists of all but which ONE of the following?
   ○ neck
   ○ greater trochanter
   ○ lesser trochanter
   ⊗ ischium

2. Which of the following is NOT part of the hip bones?
   ○ os coxae
   ⊗ trochanter
   ○ ilium
   ○ symphysis pubis

3. The socket portion of the femur ball-and-socket joint.

⊗ acetabulum
◯ patella
◯ ischium
◯ os coxae

4. Protrusions at the inferior end of the femur.

◯ medial and lateral trochanters
⊗ medial and lateral epicondyles
◯ greater and lesser trochanters
◯ greater and lesser epicondyles

5. Thigh bone.

◯ os coxae
◯ patella
⊗ femur
◯ ilium

Appendicular Skeleton – Lower Leg and Foot

The lower legs, ankle, feet, and toes are the last part of the lower extremities. Like the hands and fingers, there are many small bones that allow mobility and flexibility. Running, jumping, climbing, and walking are made possible by the amazing lower extremity bone structure. These bones include the tibia, fibula, tarsals, metatarsals, and phalanges.

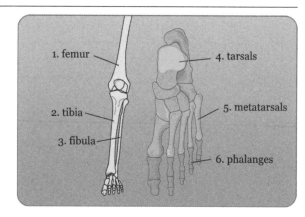

Tibia

The tibia is the largest of the two lower leg bones. It connects with the femur to form the knee joint and is located on the medial (big toe) side of the leg. The tibia has a sharp, bony ridge that runs lengthwise down the center of the shaft to form the shinbone (which can be felt through the skin on the front of the leg). The most distal point of the tibia forms the medial malleolus, or ankle bone. This protrudes sharply and can be felt on the inner side of the ankle joint. The tibia is the weight-bearing bone of the lower leg.

Fibula

The fibula is a long, skinny lower leg bone that looks rather fragile. It is situated on the lateral (little toe) side of the leg. It is not a weight-bearing bone. The proximal end of the fibula forms the lateral part of the knee joint, and the distal end forms the lateral malleolus, which protects the lateral portion of the ankle.

Tarsals, Metatarsals, and Phalanges

The tarsals are ankle bones and, along with the other bones in the foot (the metatarsals and phalanges), support weight and act as shock absorbers for the body. There are 7 tarsal bones in each foot: the talus, calcaneus, cuboid, navicular, and 1st, 2nd, and 3rd cuneiforms. The talus articulates with the tibia to bear weight from the legs. The medial malleolus (on the tibia) and the lateral malleolus (on the fibula) protect the talus on both sides.

The metatarsals are the bones of the feet and sit upon arches. There are 5 metatarsals in each foot.

The phalanges, or toes, connect to the metatarsals. There are 14 phalanges per foot—2 in the great toe, and 3 each in the remaining toes. The separations between the phalanges are identified as follows: the distal phalanx (tip of the toe), the middle phalanx (in the middle), and the proximal phalanx (nearest the point of connection to the metatarsals). Notice that the medical term for toes is the same as for fingers.

I. **MATCHING.**
   Match the correct term to the definition.

1.	B	metatarsals
2.	A	tarsals
3.	D	phalanges
4.	E	malleolus
5.	C	tibia

A. ankle bone(s)
B. feet bones
C. larger lower leg bone
D. toes
E. protects the ankle

II. **MULTIPLE CHOICE.**
    Choose the best answer.

1. How many phalanges are in the foot?
   - ○ 3
   - ○ 6
   - ⊗ 14
   - ○ 9

2. The more fragile of the lower leg bones.
   - ○ tibia
   - ⊗ fibula

3. The stronger and bigger of the lower leg bones.
   - ⊗ tibia
   - ○ fibula

4. Which is not a tarsal bone?

   ○ 2nd cuneiform
   ○ talus
   ○ navicular
   ⊗ epicondyle

5. Which of the following do the metatarsals rest upon?

   ○ ankles
   ○ calves
   ⊗ arches
   ○ malleolus

Appendicular Skeleton – Arches of the Foot

A segmented structure like the foot can support weight only if it is arched. Each foot has three arches: the transverse arch, the medial longitudinal arch, and the lateral longitudinal arch. These three arches maintain their strength and flexibility because of the shapes and interlocking capabilities of the bones, ligaments, and tendons of the foot and ankle.

Arches flex when bearing weight, then return to their normal shape when weight is lifted. The **lateral longitudinal arch** is a very low arch, arching just enough to redistribute some body weight to the calcaneus and the head of the fifth metatarsal. The **medial longitudinal arch** is the predominant arch in the foot. It runs from the base of the calcaneus up to the talus, and down again to the three medial metatarsals. (Note: The lateral longitudinal arch extends under the two most lateral metatarsals, and the medial arch extends under the three other metatarsals).

Highlights

Each foot has three arches:

1. transverse arch
2. medial longitudinal arch
3. lateral longitudinal arch

The above two arches create a frame for the **transverse arch** which is formed at the base of the metatarsals (between the tarsals and the metatarsals) and extends from the medial to the lateral sides of the foot. These three arches are shaped such that they are able to distribute the weight of the human body in a 50/50 ratio: half the weight is on the calcaneal bones, and the other half is on the metatarsals, which also provides for proper balance.

The **calcaneus** (heel bone) is the strongest bone in the foot. It forms the outer part of the ankle and extends back to form the heel. It acts as a shock absorber and bears the immediate stress placed on the foot while walking.

Review: Lower Appendicular Bones

I. **FILL IN THE BLANK.**
   Enter the terms in the space provided.

1. os coxae _____

2. femur _____

3. ilium _____

4. ischium _____

5. symphysis pubis _____

6. greater trochanter _____

7. lesser trochanter _____

8. acetabulum _____

9. medial epicondyle _____

10. lateral epicondyle _____

11. patella _____

12. tibia _____

13. malleolus _____

14. fibula _____

15. tarsals _____

16. talus _____

17. calcaneus _____

18. cuboid _____

19. navicular _____

20. cuneiforms _____

21. metatarsals _____

22. phalanges _____

II. TRUE/FALSE.
The following terms are spelled correctly: true or false?

1. longitudnal arch
   - ◯ true
   - ⊗ false

2. traverse arch
   - ◯ true
   - ⊗ false

3. phalanges
   - ⊗ true
   - ◯ false

4. tibula
   - ◯ true
   - ⊗ false

5. metacapral
   - ◯ true
   - ⊗ false

III. TRUE/FALSE.
Mark the following true or false.

1. Arches bend when not bearing weight.
   - ◯ true
   - ⊘ false

2. Each foot has three arches.
   - ⊗ true
   - ◯ false

3. The tarsals are knee bones.
   - ◯ true
   - ⊗ false

4. The fibula is the largest of the two lower leg bones.
   - ○ true
   - ⊗ false

5. There are 5 metatarsals in each foot.
   - ⊗ true
   - ○ false

Types of Bones

The human skeleton consists of bones of many different shapes and sizes.

I. **TERMINOLOGY.**
Enter each term in the space provided. Read the definition and description for each term.

1. **long bones** _____

Long bones are bones whose length is greater than their width, such as the bones of the extremities (tibia, fibula, femur, radius, ulna, humerus).

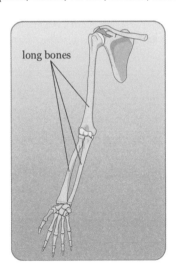

2. **short bones** _____

Short bones are shaped more like cubes and are generally found in the ankle and wrist (carpus and tarsus).

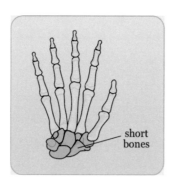

3. **flat bones** _____

Flat bones are found in the cranial vault, sternum (breastbone), shoulder blades, and ribs. Flat bones are made up of a layer of marrow (diploe) sandwiched between two layers of compact bone.

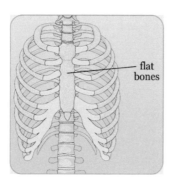

4. **irregular bones** _____

Irregular bones are a mix of irregularly shaped bones that do not fall into any of the other bone-type categories. They are found in the face, spinal column, and hips.

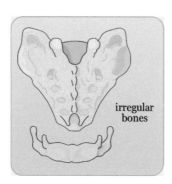

5. **sesamoid bones** _____

Sesamoid bones are mostly rounded masses embedded in certain tendons and are usually related to the surfaces of joints. Included in this group are the patella (kneecap), metacarpophalangeal joints of the hands, and metatarsophalangeal joints of the toes.

sesamoid
bones

6. **wormian bones** _____

Wormian bones are small bones found between suture lines of the skull where the edges of the skull bones are joined together.

II. FILL IN THE BLANK.
Using the terms in the box, determine the correct type of bone for each term.

1. patella _SESAMOID_

2. ribs _FLAT_

3. ankle _SHORT_

4. femur _LONG_

5. fused skull bones _WORMIAN_

6. shoulder blades _FLAT_

7. humerus _LONG_

8. wrist _SHORT_

9. hips _IRREGULAR_

10. face _IRREGULAR_

long
short
flat
irregular
sesamoid
wormian

Joints and Articulations

A joint is an area where two or more bones come together. This contact point creates an important relationship with respect to the body's ability to move. If any of the bones in a joint do not function properly, the joint will not be able to operate as a unit (not all joints, however, are made for movement). There are three kinds of joints: fibrous joints (nonmoveable), cartilaginous joints (somewhat moveable), and synovial joints (very moveable).

Term	Definition	Example
fibrous joints	No joint cavity and, in general, does not move.	radioulnar and tibiofibular joints
cartilaginous joints	Has no cavity and is somewhat moveable.	growth zones in the arms and legs
synovial joints	Joint cavity which is kept lubricated by synovial fluid.	intercarpal joint

Fibrous Joints

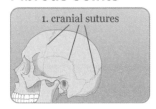

1. cranial sutures

There are two types of fibrous joints: suture and syndesmosis. A fibrous joint has no joint cavity and, in general, does not move. Examples of fibrous joints include cranial sutures and the radioulnar and tibiofibular joints.

Cartilaginous Joints

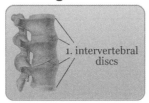

1. intervertebral discs

There are two types of cartilaginous joints: synchondrosis and symphysis. Although a cartilaginous joint has no cavity, it is still somewhat moveable. Examples of cartilaginous joints are the growth zones in the arms and legs and the discs between the vertebrae.

Synovial Joints

There are four types of synovial joints: plane, uniaxial, biaxial, and multiaxial. A synovial joint has a joint cavity which is kept lubricated by synovial fluid. The looser the joint, the more unstable and susceptible it is to injury or other damage. The body compensates for the weakness in synovial joints with ligaments, tendons, and muscle overlays. In this way, joints can be strengthened and supported to a much higher degree, yet still be capable of functioning freely.

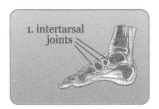

1. intertarsal joints

Plane joints are joints that glide where the flat ends of bones connect. Examples of plane joints are the intercarpal and intertarsal joints.

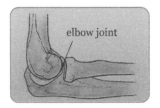

elbow joint

Uniaxial joints allow movement around one axis only. Examples of uniaxial joints are the elbow joint and the interphalangeal joint.

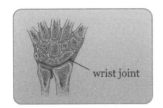

Biaxial joints allow movement around two axes. Examples of biaxial joints are the knee joint, the temporomandibular (jaw) joint, and the radiocarpal (wrist) joint.

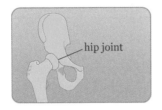

Multiaxial joints allow movement around three axes. Examples of multiaxial joints are the ball and socket joint found in the hip and shoulder, as well as the carpometacarpal joint of the thumb between the trapezium (base of thumb) and the first metacarpal. Ball and socket joints are the most freely moveable joints in the body.

Joint Names

To review, a **joint** is a place of union or a junction between two or more bones of the skeleton. It can also be made up of a specific part of a bone, or part of a bone and another bone. Each joint in the body has a specific name. Generally, the name is derived from the parts that make up the joint and are joined together into one word with the use of the connector *o*. Occasionally a dictator will join several terms together that can be viewed or spoken about as one unit. An example of this would be cervicothoracolumbar spine. However, there are also times when a dictator joins together elements that cannot possibly be either seen or used together, such as discussed earlier with carpometatarsal. Be aware of this and confirm in a dictionary or word list the existence of a term you have never heard before, or at least make sure that such elements adjoin in the body.

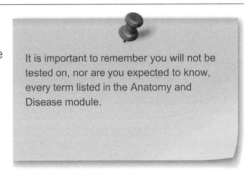

It is important to remember you will not be tested on, nor are you expected to know, every term listed in the Anatomy and Disease module.

In medical terminology, the vowel *o* is used to join other structures besides just bones. This concept should be very familiar to you from your work in the Medical Word Building module. In most joints, the contacting surfaces of the bones are protected with layers of cartilage. Cartilage is a specialized fibrous connective tissue that is vital in both the development and growth of bones. Some of the terms in this list are made up of one or more types of cartilage. Some of the terms listed below describe junctions of bone with cartilage, as well as one piece or type of cartilage with another.

The purpose of these exercises is not that you memorize every term on these lists. However, because spelling is important, some exercises involve recognizing whether or not a term is spelled correctly. This module of the program is intended primarily for the introduction of terms commonly used in medical transcription and for reference.

Following is a list of common articulations. Generally these words will be dictated and followed by the word *joint* or *junction*. This is by no means a complete list. Be sure to verify anything that is not familiar or found below when you begin transcribing.

I. FILL IN THE BLANK.
Enter the term in the space provided.

1. acromioclavicular _____
2. atlantoaxial _____
3. calcaneocuboid _____
4. carpometacarpal _____
5. costochondral _____
6. costovertebral _____
7. cricoarytenoid _____
8. cricothyroid _____
9. cubitoradial _____
10. cuneocuboid _____
11. cuneonavicular _____
12. glenohumeral _____
13. humeroradial _____
14. humeroulnar _____
15. iliofemoral _____
16. iliosacral _____
17. incudomalleolar _____
18. incudostapedial _____
19. intercarpal _____
20. interphalangeal _____
21. manubriosternal _____
22. metacarpophalangeal _____
23. patellofemoral _____
24. radiocarpal _____
25. radioulnar _____
26. sacroiliac _____
27. sternoclavicular _____
28. talonavicular _____
29. tarsometatarsal _____
30. temporomandibular _____
31. tibiofibular _____

II. SPELLING.
Determine if the following words are spelled correctly. If the spelling is correct, leave the word as it has already been entered. If the spelling is incorrect, provide the correct spelling.

1. costvertebral _COSTOVERTEBRAL_
2. humoulnar _HUMEROULNAR_
3. manubriosternal _✓_
4. iliosacral _✓_
✗ 5. carpometarsal _CARPOMETACARPAL_
6. crycoaritenoid _CRICOARYTENOID_
7. radioulnar _✓_
8. cricothyroid _✓_
9. incudostapediel _INCUDOSTAPEDIAL_
10. glenohumoral _GLENOHUMERAL_

126

III. TRUE/FALSE.
The following words are spelled correctly: true or false?

1. atlantoaxal
   - ○ true
   - ⊗ false

2. talonavicular
   - ⊗ true
   - ○ false

3. cubidoradial
   - ○ true
   - ⊗ false

4. intercarpal
   - ⊗ true
   - ○ false

5. sacroiliac
   - ⊗ true
   - ○ false

6. ileofemoral
   - ○ true
   - ⊗ false

7. cuniocuboid
   - ○ true
   - ⊗ false

8. radiocarpal
   - ⊗ true
   - ○ false

9. patellofemoral
   - ⊗ true
   - ○ false

10. temporomandibuler
    - ○ true
    - ⊗ false

Joint Movement – Lesson 1

Along with the many different types of joints in the body, there are many different ways in which joints move. These are often noted in the physical examination of patients with aches, pains, and difficulty with movement.

Take a moment to try each of these joint movements. What are you doing when you pick up a gallon of milk? What about when you reach for an item from a high shelf?

I. **TERMINOLOGY.**
   Enter each term in the space provided. Read the definition and description for each term.

   1. **flexion** _____
   Bending to decrease the angle between two bones. Think of this as flexing the biceps.

   2. **extension** _____
   Unbending to increase the angle between two bones. Think of this as extending, as in reaching your arm as far as you can (virtually eliminating the angle between the humerus and the radius/ulna).

   3. **abduction** _____
   Moving a body part away from the midline.

   4. **adduction** _____
   Moving a body part towards the midline. (Think of this as adding a body part back to the body.)

   5. **circumduction** _____
   Movement of a body part in a circle, which can include all the above joint movements as well.

II. **MATCHING.**
   Match the correct term to the definition.

   1. _E_ extension
   2. _B_ flexion
   3. _C_ abduction
   4. _D_ adduction
   5. _A_ circumduction

   A. circling
   B. bending
   C. moving away from midline
   D. adding a part back to the body
   E. unbending

III. **FILL IN THE BLANK.**
    Use the word(s) in the box to fill in the blanks.

    1. Moving your hand into a fist is considered ___FLEXION___ .

    2. While sitting in a chair with your feet flat on the ground, straighten your leg. This is ___EXTENSION___ .

    3. A great back stretch would be bending from the waist toward the right, and circling all the way around. This is called

       ___CIRCUMDUCTION___

    4. ___EXTENSION___ would be used in straightening your arm.

    5. ___FLEXION___ would be used in folding your arms.

| circumduction |
| flexion |
| adduction |
| extension |

Joint Movement – Lesson 2

I. **TERMINOLOGY.**
   Enter each term in the space provided. Read the definition and description for each term.

   1. **rotation** _____
   Movement of a body part or parts around its axis.

   2. **supine** _____
   The position of the body when lying face up, including hands being palm up and feet bent upwards.

   3. **prone** _____
   The position of the body when lying face down, including the hands being palm down and the feet bent downwards.

   4. **dorsiflexion** _____
   Movement of the foot that brings the top of the foot closer to the leg.

   5. **plantar flexion** _____
   Movement of the foot that brings the heel closer to the posterior part of the leg, the toe pointed farther away from the leg.

II. MATCHING.
Match the correct term to the definition.

1. _D_ dorsiflexion
2. _C_ plantar flexion
3. _E_ rotation
4. _B_ supine
5. _A_ prone

A. lying face down
B. lying face up
C. pointing the toe
D. flexing the foot
E. around an axis

III. FILL IN THE BLANK.
Use the word(s) in the box to fill in the blanks.

1. Lying face down, as necessary for back surgery, is considered _PRONE_ .

2. _ROTATION_ is movement around an axis or stationary point.

3. In a chorus line, dancers must always use _PLANTAR FLEXION_

4. In karate, in order to avoid breaking the toes, an athlete must use _DORSIFLEXION_

5. Surgery on the chest cavity would require the patient to be placed in _SUPINE_ .

plantar flexion

supine

prone

rotation

dorsiflexion

IV. MULTIPLE CHOICE.
Select the best answer.

1. Dorsiflexion is _____.
   - ○ movement of the foot that brings the heel closer to the posterior part of the leg
   - ○ movement of a body part in a circle
   - ○ movement of a body part on its axis
   - ⊗ movement of the foot that brings the top of the foot closer to the leg

2. Synovial joints _____.
   - ○ rarely move
   - ⊗ move with ease
   - ○ never move
   - ○ only move from the hips

3. Bending to decrease the angle between bones is called _____.

   ○ extension
   ○ abduction
   ⊗ flexion
   ○ plantar flexion

4. Circumduction is _____.

   ○ movement on the axis
   ⊗ movement in a circle
   ○ movement towards the midline
   ○ unbending to increase the angle between two bones

5. The position of the body when lying face down, including the hands being palm down and the feet bent downwards, is called _____.

   ○ rested
   ⊗ prone
   ○ flat
   ○ supine

6. An area where two bones move is called a _____.

   ○ suture
   ⊗ joint
   ○ synovial
   ○ facet

7. The three types of joints are _____.

   ○ fibrous, fractured, synovial
   ○ synovial, cartilaginous, simple
   ⊗ fibrous, cartilaginous, synovial
   ○ syndesmosis, cartilaginous, fibrous

8. Plane joints are _____.

   ○ cartilaginous joints
   ○ fibrous joints
   ⊗ synovial joints
   ○ symphysis joints

9. Joints that allow movement around three axes are called _____.

  ○ uniaxial
  ⊗ triaxial
  ○ biaxial
  ○ multiaxial

10. Cartilaginous joints are _____.

  ○ freely moveable
  ⊗ somewhat moveable
  ○ generally not moveable
  ○ moveable only by a medical professional

Bone/Muscle Attachment

On the surface of bones exist both depressions and projections in order for muscles to attach to bone, bone to attach to muscle, or to allow nerves/blood supply a pathway. A process is a **projection** from a bone. A cavity/opening in a bone is called a **depression**.

Projections	Example
tubercle	Small, rounded process on the femur.
trochanter	Massive and found only on the femur.
condyle	Round, articulating knob on the humerus.
tuberosity	Large, rounded process on the humerus.
Depression	Example
fossa	Flattened, shallow; i.e. armpit (axillae).
sulcus	Grooved, fissure; i.e. deep furrows of brain.
sinus	Cavity, hollow space in bone.
foramen	Allows nerves and blood vessels to pass; i.e. foramen of skull.

I. **FILL IN THE BLANK.**
   Enter the term in the space provided.

1. tubercle_____   2. trochanter_____

3. condyle_____   4. tuberosity_____

5. fossa_____   6. sulcus_____

7. sinus_____   8. foramen_____

II. TRUE/FALSE.
Determine if the following are true or false.

1. A fossa is a projection from bone.
   - ( ) true
   - (⊗) false

2. A sinus is a depression in bone.
   - (⊗) true
   - ( ) false

3. A foramen is a depression in bone.
   - ( ) true
   - (⊗) false

4. A condyle is a depression in bone.
   - ( ) true
   - (⊗) false

5. A tuberosity is both a projection and depression.
   - ( ) true
   - (⊗) false

Ligaments

The ligaments are closely related to the skeletal system and vital to the function of it. They are specifically associated with joints. A **ligament** is a band of white, fibrous, slightly elastic tissue that binds the ends of bones together. This binding prevents dislocations and stress that can cause fractures.

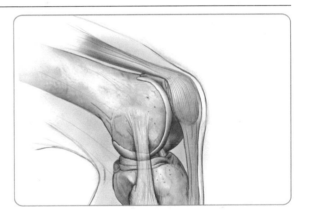

The word *ligament* comes from the Latin word *ligamentum* meaning to band or tie. A ligament made up of many fibrous bands is called a **collateral ligament**.

Most ligaments derive their names from the area where they are located, their shape, or the bones and/or structures near that area. For example, there is a carpal ligament in the wrist and a series of cervical ligaments in the neck, which are terms that, by now, should be somewhat familiar to you.

Because of the repetition that occurs in the naming of individual ligaments, there is no reason to map out and memorize each and every individual ligament in the body. Instead, we will deal specifically with two types of ligaments.

1. Ligaments that are susceptible to injury.
2. Ligaments that are studied in common injuries and the terms that are related to them.

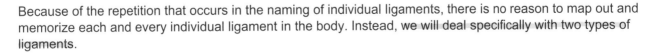

There are many ligaments that are not listed here. As you become more familiar with human anatomy, most of the ligaments will become familiar to you as well. You will be able to recognize the names as similar to the names of surrounding structures, shapes, and positions (such as anterior or lateral).

I. TERMINOLOGY.
Enter each term in the space provided. Read the definition and description for each term.

1. **accessory ligament** _____

Any ligament that strengthens or supports another ligament.

2. **arcuate ligament** _____

Means yellow ligaments; they are located in the spine and assist in maintaining the erect position. (Also called ligamenta flava [plural], and ligamentum flavum [singular].)

3. **collateral ligament** _____

There are several types of collateral ligaments, including fibular, radial, tibial, ulnar, etc. These are basically ligaments that are not direct, but are supporting ligaments.

4. **coracoid ligament** _____

Coracoid means like a raven's beak and is used to describe an area on the scapula. It is so named for its shape.

5. **cruciate ligament** _____

Cruciate means shaped like a cross. There are different types of cruciate ligaments, including anterior, posterior, and lateral. They appear in many places in human anatomy, such as the knees, fingers, and toes.

6. **falciform ligament** _____

Falciform means shaped like a sickle and appears near the sacral tuberosity as well as within the liver.

7. **inguinal ligament** _____

Inguinal is a term used to describe the groin area.

8. **interosseous ligament** _____

Interosseous means between bones and describes several different ligaments.

9. **longitudinal ligament** _____

Longitudinal simply means lengthwise. It is used to describe any ligament that runs lengthwise.

10. **nuchal ligament** _____

Nuchal means pertaining to the neck.

11. **triquetral ligament** _____

Triquetral means three cornered and appears in different places throughout the body. The prefix tri- should be familiar as meaning three.

II. MATCHING.
Match the correct term to the definition.

1. A cruciate
2. E arcuate
3. B accessory
4. D coracoid
5. C collateral

A. shaped like a cross
B. support
C. indirect
D. like a raven's beak
E. yellow ligament

III. FILL IN THE BLANK.
Use the word(s) in the box to fill in the blanks.

1. An area of the scapula is shaped like a bird's beak. The ligament that surrounds it is called the _CORACOID_ ligament.

2. An _ACCESSORY_ ligament strengthens or supports another ligament.

3. A _CRUCIATE_ ligament is shaped like a cross.

4. Located on the spine, the _ARCUATE_ ligament literally means "yellow ligament."

5. There are several types of _COLLATERAL_ ligaments that are made up of several bands and are not directly connected.

accessory

collateral

cruciate

coracoid

arcuate

Unit 8
Sensory Organs

Sensory Organs – Introduction

The senses, which include sight, smell, taste, hearing, and touch, are important tools in relating the body and its internal systems to the external world. The anatomical parts that perform these functions are not individually or collectively part of any single system, but their role is unique and important to carry out the functions that allow for interaction between the body and the environment. Three primary sensory organs will be covered in this unit: the skin, the eye, and the ear (including the related nose and throat). The mouth is responsible for taste, but its anatomy is relatively simple and will be covered at another time.

The senses allow interaction with the external world through a variety of means: they alert us to danger, draw us to nutritional sources, allow for communication, transmit information important to cognitive functions, and enhance the overall quality of life. Without sight, one would never see a magnificent sunset; without hearing, one would not experience the exhilaration of beautiful music; without touch, one would miss the luxurious softness of a puppy's fur; without smell, one would never enjoy the scent of roses, and food would only taste half as good; and without taste, well, what would life be without chocolate? Maintaining proper function of these sensory perceptors may not be vital to the sustenance of life itself, but it does add substantially to human convenience, contentment, and quality of life.

The skin, along with the hair, nails, glands, and breasts, encompass the integumentary system. The first sensory organ we will be exploring is the skin.

Skin – Introduction

The **skin** is the largest human organ, covering approximately 3,000 square inches on an average adult. It is considered an organ because it is made up of several kinds of tissues that are structurally arranged to work together. It covers the entire external surface of the body. Along with its associated structures (hair, glands, and nails) it constitutes the integumentary system. This system accounts for approximately 7% of a body's weight and performs six important functions. These include:

1. **Protection of the body from disease and external injury**. The tough outer layer of skin is adapted to withstand abrasion and penetration of pathogens. The pigmented layer protects the body from the damaging effects of ultraviolet light.
2. **Prevention of dehydration**. The outer layer of the skin is essentially waterproof, protecting the body from desiccation (the act of drying up) on land and from absorption when immersed in water.
3. **Regulation of body temperature**. Evaporative cooling is made possible by the secretion and evaporation of perspiration. Vasoconstriction of the capillary vessels assists warming of the body while vasodilation of the capillary vessels assists in cooling.
4. **Reception of stimuli**. The skin is rich with sensory receptors specialized for touch, pressure, temperature, and pain.
5. **Regulation of body fluids**. The skin performs an excretory function to eliminate excess water, salts, or other metabolic wastes.
6. **Selective absorption**. Some substances that are beneficial to the body can penetrate through the skin, such as gases, vitamins, and hormones. This explains the effectiveness of medicinal patches.

Skin Structures – Lesson 1

The skin on cross section is pictured here with all the major structures identified. It is a good idea to become very familiar with the terms here and especially the spelling of the terms, as you will hear these terms frequently throughout the practicum portion of this training program. You might also hear these terms frequently in ER dictation (picture someone coming in with twig embedded in the dermis) or as a clinic medical transcriptionist (teenage acne—enough said?).

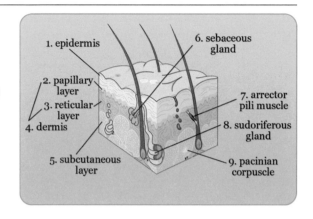

I. **TERMINOLOGY.**
   Enter each term in the space provided. Read the definition and description for each term.

1. **epidermis** _____
   Layer of tissue with no nerve supply or blood.

2. **papillary** _____
   Layer of the dermis; contains loose connective tissue.

3. **reticular** _____
   Lower layer of skin; contains thick, collagen fibers.

4. **dermis** _____
   Also called the corium, it lies directly beneath the epidermis. Hair follicles, oil glands (sebaceous), and sweat glands are located in dermis.

5. **subcutaneous** _____
   Connective tissue that contains fat (adipose tissue) and connects organs to underlying skin. Also called the hypodermis.

6. **sebaceous** _____
   Oil-secreting gland of the skin. Produces an oily substance called sebum.

7. **arrector pili** _____
   A type of smooth muscle that moves hairs.

8. **sudoriferous** _____
   Also called sweat glands, these glands open as pores on the skin's surface. Found on palms, soles, armpits (axillae), and forehead.

9. **pacinian corpuscle** _____
   Found in subcutaneous tissue, these sense touch and vibratory pressure.

II. FILL IN THE BLANK.
Label the skin properties in the corresponding boxes.

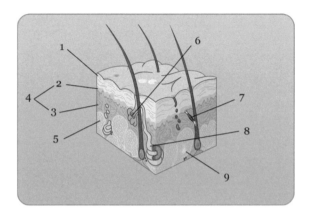

1. EPIDERMIS

2. PAPILLARY LAYER

3. RETICULAR LAYER

4. DERMIS

5. SUBCUTANEOUS LAYER

6. SEBACEOUS GLAND

7. ARRECTOR PILI MUSCLE

8. SUDORIFEROUS GLAND

9. PACINIAN CORPUSCLE

Skin Structures – Lesson 2

The outermost layer of skin, the epidermis, is composed of **stratified squamous epithelium**, which is between 20 and 30 cell layers thick. All of the epidermis (except for the very deepest layers) is composed of dead cells containing a protein called **keratin**, which toughens and waterproofs the skin. There are five sublayers that comprise the epidermis, but as a transcriptionist you will rarely come across these terms. In medical reports, the term **subcuticular** means underneath the epidermis. This term is used often when closing the skin following an operative procedure.

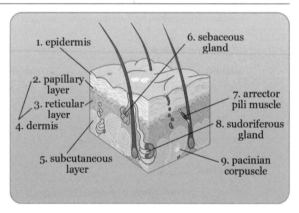

The dermis is deeper and thicker than the epidermis. It consists of collagenous, elastic, and reticular fibers. The elastic fibers are the most superficial and they provide skin tone. A young person has many more elastic fibers than an elderly person. The dermis is highly vascular, glandular, and has many nerve endings. It can be divided into two layers: the papillary and reticular layers. The papillary layer is thin and contacts the epidermis. The folds of this layer, which make up fingerprint patterns, contain touch receptors. The deeper reticular portion of the dermis contains sweat glands (sudoriferous), oil glands (sebaceous glands), and different types of nerve receptors. One of these, the pacinian corpuscle, is the most complicated nerve ending and is sensitive to pressure and vibration. These are found throughout the body.

The subcutaneous layer is composed of loose connective tissue and a lot of adipose tissue. It binds the skin to the underlying muscle and insulates and protects the body. It is considerably thicker in females than in males. Medications are often injected into this layer because there is little pain involved due to the looseness of the subcutaneous layer. This term, too, you will encounter frequently in operative reports.

The integumentary system also includes organs which originate in the skin. The two not yet covered are hair and nails. The hair can easily be seen on the diagram, originating deeper in the skin and jetting out from the top of it. The primary function of hair is protection. Hair on the scalp and eyebrows protects against sunlight. The hair inside the nostrils, as well as the eyelashes, protects against airborne particles. Much like the epidermis, the growth of hair takes place within the deeper layer, and the cells die as they are pushed away. It is at this point that the hair becomes visible. Sebaceous glands and the smooth muscles called arrector pili are associated with hair. The arrector pili muscles are involuntary and respond to thermal or psychological stimuli. When these muscles contract, the hair is pulled into a vertical position, causing the phenomenon known as goose bumps or chills (or if you live in the south—maybe even chill bumps).

Nails are found on the distal ends of the fingers and the toes. They protect the digits and (in fingers) help to grasp and pick up small objects. They are formed from a hardened layer of the epidermis. An **eponychium** covers the area above the root of the nail. (Lay people call this a cuticle.) The **lunula** is the whitened crescent-shaped area near the nailbed root.

In addition to the functions mentioned above, the overall appearance of the skin and nails can aid in diagnosing problems or injuries that may be present in other systems. The color of the skin can indicate a variety of illnesses, such as pale skin during shock or anemia, flushed red skin with a fever, or the greenish hue accompanying digestive complaints. Changes in skin texture can indicate glandular or nutritional problems. Allergic reactions often result in rashes featuring noticeable changes in both color and texture. Even the wrinkling of the skin demonstrates aging or overexposure to the sun or to pathogens, such as tobacco. The same is true regarding the nails. Yellowish or split nails can indicate nutritional deficiencies, and a bluish tint to the nails is a sign of improper oxygenation of the blood.

I. **FILL IN THE BLANK.**
   Before continuing with the exercises related to the anatomy of this chapter, enter the terms which appear in the preceding paragraphs in the spaces provided below. Be sure to spell the terms correctly.

   1. stratified _____   2. squamous _____

   3. epithelium _____   4. keratin _____

   5. subcuticular _____ 6. eponychium _____

   7. desiccation _____

Review: Skin Structures

I. SPELLING.
Determine if the following words are spelled correctly. If the spelling is correct, leave the word as it has already been entered. If the spelling is incorrect, provide the correct spelling.

1. reticular   ✓

2. dermous   DERMIS

3. dessication   DESICCATION

4. arrector   ✓

5. squamious   SQUAMOUS

6. subcuticular   ✓

7. subcutaneus   SUBCUTANEOUS

8. eponichium   EPONYCHIUM

9. sudoriferous   ✓

10. epitellium   EPITHELIUM

11. epidermis   ✓

12. pappillary   PAPILLARY

13. keratine   KERATIN

14. stratified   ✓

15. sebaceous   ✓

16. corpussel   CORPUSCLE

II. MULTIPLE CHOICE.
Choose the term which best describes the statement.

1. The cuticle.
   - ⊗ eponychium
   - ○ aponychium
   - ○ eponichium
   - ○ eponhycium

2. The protein which toughens and waterproofs the skin.
   - ○ kerratin
   - ○ kerattin
   - ○ karetin
   - ⊗ keratin

3. The papillary and reticular layers.
   - ⊗ dermis
   - ○ dermous
   - ○ dirmes
   - ○ deirmis

4. An oil gland.

   ○ sebacous
   ⊗ sebaceous
   ○ sebacious
   ○ sabaceous

5. Underneath the epidermis.

   ○ subcuticuler
   ⊗ subcuticular
   ○ subcutticular
   ○ subcuiticular

6. The process of drying up.

   ○ dessication
   ○ desication
   ○ diseccation
   ⊗ desiccation

7. The uppermost layer of the dermis.

   ○ papilary
   ⊗ papillary
   ○ pappilary
   ○ papilllary

8. The outermost layer of the skin is composed of this type of cell.

   ⊗ stratified squamous epithelium
   ○ statified squamous epithelium
   ○ stratified squamus epithelium
   ○ stratified squamous epithilium

9. The lowermost layer of skin.

   ○ subcitaneous layer
   ○ subcuteneous layer
   ○ subcutaous layer
   ⊗ subcutaneous layer

10. The muscle responsible for goose bumps.

   ○ arector pili
   ⊗ arrector pili
   ○ errector pilli
   ○ erector pilli

11. This layer, along with the papillary layer, makes up the dermis.

    ○ raticular
    ○ reticullar
    ⊗ reticular
    ○ reticulor

12. Sweat gland.

    ○ suderiferous gland
    ○ soduriferous gland
    ⊗ sudoriferous gland
    ○ sudoriferus gland

13. The nerve ending responsible for recognizing vibration and pressure.

    ○ pasinian corpuscle
    ○ pasinian corpussel
    ○ pacnian corpussel
    ⊗ pacinian corpuscle

14. The outermost layer of skin.

    ⊗ epidermis
    ○ apidermis
    ○ epidermous
    ○ apidermous

Skin Disease Processes – Introduction

The skin is unique in the examination and the diagnosis of pathology because it is, for the most part, visible. Unlike other systems and organs, which require the presence of somatic symptoms and complaints, laboratory testing, and x-ray to determine what is wrong, the skin can be seen and problems with it can be delineated by the naked eye. A physician or other healthcare worker is usually able to examine the skin physically and decide what is causing any abnormality. For example, with chickenpox, the size, shape, distribution, and color of the rash easily defines the disease.

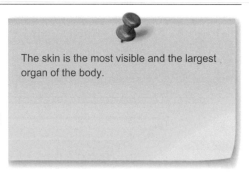

The skin is the most visible and the largest organ of the body.

Because of the unique relationship of the integumentary system to the overall function and makeup of the human body, the appearance of the skin, hair, and nails is a major way that diagnosis is made, and the symptoms almost exclusively involve various lesions that erupt on the epidermis. These lesions vary significantly in appearance: size, shape, color, texture, and depth. They can also be indicative of problems generated in other systems or related to them.

Skin is resilient and able to repair itself so that it can continue to thrive throughout the years. Of all the body's structures, the skin probably gets the most attention. Aesthetically, the skin (its color, youth, vigor, and beauty) is the focus of a multi-billion dollar cosmetics industry. Externally, the skin is exposed to the environment, chemicals, cuts, scrapes, bumps, and so on. Coupled with the fact that the skin is the body's largest organ, there are many things that can go awry. These abnormalities and disorders will be focused on over the next several pages.

Skin Abnormalities – Lesson 1

In order to understand the diseases that cause such lesions, you must first learn the names and types of skin abnormalities that often occur. Many of these terms will be commonly seen in transcription, but it is not necessary for you to be able to distinguish between the minute differences outlined below.

I. **TERMINOLOGY.**
   Enter each term in the space provided. Read the definition and description for each term.

1. **abrasion** _____

The wearing away of the epidermis by a scraping movement.

2. **blister** _____

A thin-walled sac containing serous (clear) fluid.

3. **bleb** _____

A blister-like structure filled with serous fluid.

4. **bulla** _____

A blister on the skin, greater than 5 mm in diameter, with thin walls filled with fluid. (Plural of bulla is bullae.)

5. **callus** _____

A localized buildup of layers of the epidermis caused by increased pressure or friction. A corn is a type of callus which is localized to the foot (especially around the toes).

6. **cicatrix** _____

A scar. The new tissue which forms during healing of a wound.

7. **comedo** _____

A noninflammatory lesion of acne, consisting of a plug of keratin within a dilated hair follicle. (Plural is comedones.)

8. **contusion** _____

A bruise, specifically an injury to the skin caused by blunt trauma that does not break the skin.

II. SPELLING.

Determine if the following words are spelled correctly. If the spelling is correct, leave the word as it has already been entered. If the spelling is incorrect, provide the correct spelling.

1. blib __BLEB__

2. abrasion __✓__

3. commedo __COMEDO__

4. bula __BULLA__

5. sicatrix __CICATRIX__

III. MULTIPLE CHOICE.

Choose the best answer.

1. A localized buildup of layers of skin, caused by pressure or friction.
   - ○ calus
   - ○ callous
   - ○ calous
   - ⊗ callus

2. A plug of keratin within a dilated hair follicle.
   - ○ commedo
   - ○ comido
   - ○ comeido
   - ⊗ comedo

3. An injury caused by blunt trauma.
   - ⊗ contusion
   - ○ contussion
   - ○ cuntusion
   - ○ contosion

4. A thin-walled sac containing serous fluid, greater than 5 mm in diameter.
   - ○ bula
   - ○ boula
   - ⊗ bulla
   - ○ blulla

5. A scar.
   - ○ ciccatrix
   - ⊗ cicatrix
   - ○ cecitrix
   - ○ cicitrix

Skin Abnormalities – Lesson 2

I. TERMINOLOGY.
Enter each term in the space provided. Read the definition and description for each term.

1. **ecchymosis** _____

Hemorrhage under the epidermis that causes red or purple discoloration; a bruise.

2. **eschar** _____

The crust that forms over a burn or gangrene.

3. **excoriation** _____

A scratch; a linear or hollowed-out crusted area caused by scratching, rubbing, or picking.

4. **furuncle** _____

Also called a boil, this is a painful localized bacterial infection that originates in a hair follicle or gland in the subcutaneous tissue.

5. **lichenification** _____

Localized thickening and coarsening of the skin due to chronic irritation. This is usually caused by scratching an area for a prolonged period of time.

6. **macule** _____

A flat discolored spot less than 1 cm in diameter. Macules may be of various shapes. The skin is discolored but is not different in texture or elevation from the surrounding skin. Freckles, flat moles, and tattoos are examples of macules. If the area is larger than 1 cm it is called a patch.

7. **nevus** _____

Any congenital lesion of the skin or, in other words, a birthmark. (Plural is nevi.)

8. **papule** _____

A solid elevated lesion of skin less than 1 cm in diameter. This is a superficial lesion which may or may not be of different texture and color than the surrounding skin. If the raised area is larger than 1 cm, more firm, and deeper it is called a nodule. If it is quite large, elevated, and firm it is called a tumor.

II. SPELLING.
Determine if the following words are spelled correctly. If the spelling is correct, leave the word as it has already been entered. If the spelling is incorrect, provide the correct spelling.

1. licenification _LICHENIFICATION_

2. papule _✓_

3. esckar _ESCHAR_

4. echymosis _ECCHYMOSIS_

5. nevous _NEVUS_

III. MULTIPLE CHOICE.
Choose the best answer.

1. A bruise.
   - ◯ echymosis
   - ⊗ ecchymosis
   - ◯ eccymosis
   - ◯ ecchimosis

2. An elevated lesion less than 1 cm in diameter.
   - ⊗ papule
   - ◯ pappule
   - ◯ papulle
   - ◯ papille

3. The crust which forms over a burn.
   - ◯ S-scar
   - ⊗ eschar
   - ◯ escchar
   - ◯ escar

4. A boil.
   - ◯ faruncle
   - ◯ furbuncle
   - ◯ farbuncle
   - ⊗ furuncle

5. A birthmark.
   - ◯ nevvus
   - ◯ nevius
   - ⊗ nevus
   - ◯ neivus

Skin Abnormalities – Lesson 3

I. TERMINOLOGY.
Enter each term in the space provided. Read the definition and description for each term.

1. **petechia** _____

A pinpoint, round, nonraised purplish/red spot caused by hemorrhage just beneath the epidermal layer. (Plural is petechiae.)

2. **pruritus** _____

Itching.

3. **psoriatic arthritis** _____

a chronic disease characterized by inflammation of the skin and joints

4. **purpura** _____

A small hemorrhage, up to about 1 cm, in the skin, causing purplish discoloration. This can be either macular (flat) or papular (raised).

5. **pustule** _____

A visible collection of pus in or underneath the epidermis, usually in a hair follicle or sweat pore. The pimples characteristic of acne are pustules.

6. **telangiectasia** _____

The permanent dilatation of blood vessels; causes small red lesions, visible through the skin.

7. **verrucae** _____

Warts. These are common epithelial lesions with a horny surface which are caused by human papillomavirus. They are often contagious. (Singular is verruca.) The most common form is verruca vulgaris.

8. **wheal** _____

A hive. A temporary elevated lesion caused by local edema. They usually appear suddenly and in large quantities and are a common allergic reaction.

II. SPELLING.
Determine if the following words are spelled correctly. If the spelling is correct, leave the word as it has already been entered. If the spelling is incorrect, provide the correct spelling.

1. veruccae _____✓_____   2. puritis _____PRURITUS_____

3. purpura _____✓_____   4. wheel _____WHEAL_____

5. petechea ___PETECHIA___   6. soriatic ___PSORIATIC___

III. MULTIPLE CHOICE.
Choose the best answer.

1. Permanent dilatation of the blood vessels, visible through the skin.
   - ○ telangectiasia
   - ○ telangiectasa
   - ⊗ telangiectasia
   - ○ tellangiectasia

2. A hive.
   - ○ weal
   - ⊗ wheal
   - ○ wheel
   - ○ wheale

3. Warts.
   - ○ verucae
   - ○ veruccae
   - ○ verruccae
   - ⊗ verrucae

4. Itching.
   - ⊗ pruritus
   - ○ pruritis
   - ○ puritis
   - ○ puritus

5. A pinpoint, round spot caused by hemorrhage.
   - ○ petichia
   - ○ pitechia
   - ⊗ petechia
   - ○ peteichia

Integumentary System Disorders – Lesson 1

The presence of one or more lesions or a combination of different types of lesions can be the result of many different diseases, conditions, or reactions. These are caused by allergens, imbalances, bacteria, viruses, trauma, or other substances, such as metals or rubber. Although most skin conditions are not life threatening, they can be extremely uncomfortable, irritating, and painful. Some of these, such as chickenpox, will run a course and then disappear on their own. Others require oral medication to treat the underlying pathology. However, many dermatologic complications can be treated locally, by applying salves and ointments to the affected areas.

The integumentary system, like virtually every system in the body, undergoes changes due to aging. Many of these changes, such as wrinkling, hair loss, freckling, and age spots, are asymptomatic and irreversible. They are obvious upon visualization but cause neither illness nor discomfort. Plastic surgery is the only way to treat such problems, and this is done primarily to enhance self-image and not for medical necessity. Additionally, age and specifically consistent, life-long exposure to the sun can lead to skin cancer, which is the most common type of cancer afflicting the human body. Fortunately, most skin cancers are also highly curable. On the following several pages are listings of the most common integumentary system disorders.

I. TERMINOLOGY.
    Enter each term in the space provided. Read the definition and description for each term.

1. **abscess** _____

A localized collection of pus buried in tissues, organs, or confined spaces.

2. **acne** _____

A common inflammatory disease of the sebaceous glands characterized by comedones, papules, pustules, inflamed nodules, pus-filled cysts, and, in extreme cases, deep, inflamed, purulent sacs.

3. **actinic keratosis** _____

Sharply outlined red or skin-colored, flat or raised keratotic lesions which may develop into squamous cell carcinoma.

4. **alopecia** _____

Baldness. The absence of hair in places where it should be present.

5. **basal cell carcinoma** _____

A type of skin cancer, the presentation of which varies. It can appear as small, shiny, formed nodules, ulcerated and crusty lesions, scar-like plaques, or lesions appearing like a dermatitis. The most common form begins as a small, shiny papule, gets bigger and begins to show a shiny, pearl-like border with telangiectasis. It rarely metastasizes, but does invade normal tissues.

6. **burn** _____

Injury to integumentary tissue caused by contact with fire, steam, hot liquid, chemicals, electricity, friction, or radiant exposure. It is classified by degrees: first degree burns involve redness of the superficial layers of the skin; second degree burns have blisters which involve the deeper layers of the skin; and third degree burns destroy the skin and cause damage to underlying tissues.

7. **candidiasis** _____

Infection by the Candida fungus. This is usually superficial and most commonly affects the skin. However, it also affects moist mucous areas, such as those found in the mouth, vagina, and respiratory tract.

8. **cellulitis** _____

An acute, diffuse, spreading, edematous inflammation primarily of the deep subcutaneous tissues, but sometimes affecting deeper tissues and muscles. This is often associated with abscess formation.

9. **dandruff** _____

Dry, scaly material shed from the scalp.

10. **decubitus ulcer** _____

Decubitus means literally the act of lying down. A decubitus ulcer is a bedsore, or a loss of the epidermis in patches caused by lying in bed for long periods of time.

II. **SPELLING.**
Determine if the following words are spelled correctly. If the spelling is correct, leave the word as it has already been entered. If the spelling is incorrect, provide the correct spelling.

1. acne _____✓_____   2. actinic keritosis _ACTINIC KERATOSIS_

3. basil cell carcinoma _BASAL CELL_   4. burn _____✓_____
   CARCINOMA

5. dandriff _DANDRUFF_

152

III. MULTIPLE CHOICE.
Choose the best answer.

1. Baldness is also called _____.

   ○ alopesia
   ⊗ alopecia
   ○ alopeicia
   ○ allopecia

2. An infection by the Candida fungus is _____.

   ○ candadiasis
   ○ candidasis
   ○ candodiasis
   ⊗ candidiasis

3. A localized collection of pus is an _____.

   ⊗ abscess
   ○ abcess
   ○ absess
   ○ absces

4. An acute edematous inflammation is called _____.

   ⊗ cellulitis
   ○ celulitis
   ○ cellulites
   ○ cellulytis

5. A bedsore is called a_____.

   ○ decubeitus ulcer
   ⊗ decubitus ulcer
   ○ decubotus ulcer
   ○ dequibitus ulcer

Integumentary System Disorders – Lesson 2

I. TERMINOLOGY.
Enter each term in the space provided. Read the definition and description for each term.

1. **dermatitis** _____

Inflammation of the skin. There are several different types of dermatitis. Some of these are included below.

2. **atopic dermatitis** _____

A chronic itching, superficial inflammation of the skin usually associated with a family history of related disorders, such as hayfever and asthma.

3. **contact dermatitis** _____

Acute or chronic dermatitis caused by materials or substances that come into contact with the skin.

4. **nummular dermatitis** _____

Chronic dermatitis in which there are inflamed, coin-shaped, crusted and scaling pruritic lesions.

5. **seborrheic dermatitis** _____

An inflammatory scaling disease of the scalp, face, and sometimes other areas. Sometimes used synonymously with dandruff.

6. **stasis dermatitis** _____

The persistent inflammation of the skin of the lower legs with a tendency to have brown pigment. This is associated with venous insufficiency.

7. **dermatofibroma** _____

Also called fibrous histiocytoma, this refers to a firm, red or brown, small papule or nodule occurring in the dermis. This is commonly seen in the legs of women following minor trauma.

8. **histiocytoma** _____

Also known as dermatofibroma.

9. **eczema** _____

This term is sometimes used synonymously with dermatitis, and sometimes to specify atopic dermatitis. It means literally "oozing or weeping," and is characterized by pruritic papules with oozing, crusting, and scaling, and secondarily by lichenification of the affected skin.

10. **erythema** _____

By itself this means redness of the skin. There are two specific types which are commonly seen in dermatology. These are: erythema multiforme and erythema nodosum.

II. SPELLING.
Determine if the following words are spelled correctly. If the spelling is correct, leave the word as it has already been entered. If the spelling is incorrect, provide the correct spelling.

1. stassis   STASIS   2. dermatitis   ✓

3. ezcema   ECZEMA   4. nummular   ✓

5. erethyma   ERYTHEMA

III. TRUE/FALSE.
Mark the following true or false.

1. Nummular dermatitis is usually caused by hayfever or asthma.

   ○ true
   ⊗ false

2. Seborrheic dermatitis is used synonymously with eczema.

   ○ true
   ⊗ false

3. Dermatitis is an inflammation of the skin.

   ⊗ true
   ○ false

4. Histiocytoma is commonly seen in the legs of women following minor trauma.

   ⊗ true
   ○ false

5. Hayfever or asthma can cause atopic dermatitis.

   ○ true
   ⊗ false

Integumentary System Disorders – Lesson 3

I. TERMINOLOGY.
Enter each term in the space provided. Read the definition and description for each term.

1. **erythema multiforme** _____

An inflammatory eruption of the skin with symmetric, red, bullous lesions.

2. **erythema nodosum** _____

An inflammatory disease of the skin and subcutaneous tissue characterized by tender red nodules, especially in the tibial region, but also involving the arms and other areas.

3. **folliculitis** _____

Inflammation of a follicle or follicles. This generally refers to hair follicles.

4. **gangrene** _____

The death of tissue (necrosis), usually affecting a large area; associated with loss of vascular supply and secondarily with bacterial infection and putrefaction (decomposition).

5. **putrefaction** _____

Enzymatic decomposition, especially of proteins, with the production of foul-smelling compounds.

6. **hemangioma** _____

Localized benign vascular tumors of the skin and subcutaneous tissues.

7. **hidradenitis suppurativa** _____

A recurrent skin disease, characterized by boil-like lesions or abscesses, usually found around hair follicles and apocrine sweat glands.

8. **ichthyosis** _____

Any of several skin disorders in which the skin is dry and scaly.

9. **ichthyosis vulgaris** _____

The most common type of ichthyosis is ichthyosis vulgaris, which is characterized by prominent scaling on the extensor surfaces of the extremities and the back. Interestingly, flexor surfaces, the abdomen and face, are usually spared. "Ichthys" means "fish," and the condition resembles fish scales.

10. **impetigo** _____

A superficial vesiculopustular infection of the skin most frequently caused by Staphylococcus aureus. The most commonly affected areas are the arms, legs, and face.

II. **SPELLING.**
   Determine if the following words are spelled correctly. If the spelling is correct, leave the word as it has already been entered. If the spelling is incorrect, provide the correct spelling.

1. nodisum _NODOSUM_

2. putrifaction _PUTREFACTION_

3. hemangioma _HEMANGIOMA_

4. hydradenitis supurativa _HIDRADENITIS SUPPURATIVA_

5. impitigo _IMPETIGO_

III. FILL IN THE BLANK.
Using the word/word parts in the box, fill in the blanks.

1. The death of tissue usually affecting a large area.

   GANGRENE

2. Benign vascular tumors of the skin and subcutaneous tissue.

   HEMANGIOMA

3. Inflammation of a follicle. FOLLICULITIS

4. Inflammatory eruption of the skin with symmetric, red, bullous

   lesions. ERYTHEMA MULTIFORME

5. Dry skin is also known as this. ICHTHYOSIS

erythema multiforme
folliculitis
gangrene
ichthyosis
hemangioma

Integumentary System Disorders – Lesson 4

I. TERMINOLOGY.
Enter each term in the space provided. Read the definition and description for each term.

1. **Kaposi sarcoma** _____

A neoplasm characterized by bluish-red skin nodules found most often on the lower extremities (especially the feet) which increase in size and number and spread to more proximal sites. This disease is endemic to Central Africa and Central and Eastern Europe, and a particularly virulent form occurs in patients with acquired immune deficiency syndrome (AIDS).

2. **keloid** _____

An enlarged or overgrown (hypertrophic) scar. Keloids are shiny, smooth, dome-shaped, and slightly pink.

3. **keratoacanthoma** _____

A round, firm, usually flesh-colored lesion with a central crater containing keratinous material.

4. **melanoma** _____

A tumor arising from the melanocytic system of the skin. If the term is used alone, it refers to malignant melanoma. Melanomas vary in size, shape, color (although they are usually pigmented), and in their propensity to invade and metastasize. Such a tumor can spread so quickly that it is fatal within a few months.

5. **mycosis fungoides** _____

A malignant condition in which itchy and erythematous patches gradually evolve into plaques infiltrated by abnormal lymphocytes and convoluted nuclei and then onto the tumor stage.

6. **paronychia** _____

Infection at the margin of a nail.
Also onychia: Infection of the nailbed.

7. **pediculosis** _____

Infestation with lice. Pediculus is the genus of sucking lice, and is therefore capitalized. This can affect the head (Pediculus humanus capitis), the body (Pediculus humanus corporis), or the genitals (Phthirus pubis).

8. **pityriasis rosea** _____

A self-limiting, mild inflammatory skin disease characterized by scaly lesions.

9. **psoriasis** _____

A common chronic and recurrent disease characterized by dry, silvery, scaling papules of various sizes.

10. **pyoderma** _____

A general term for any skin condition caused by pus-forming bacteria.

II. SPELLING.
Determine if the following words are spelled correctly. If the spelling is correct, leave the word as it has already been entered. If the spelling is incorrect, provide the correct spelling.

1. kapposi sarcoma _KAPOSI SARCOMA_   2. mycosis fungoides _✓_

3. melinoma _MELANOMA_   4. pityriasis rosia _PITYRIASIS ROSEA_

5. psoriasis _✓_

III. MATCHING.
Match the term to the definition.

1. _B_ Infection at the margin of a nail.

2. _E_ An enlarged and overgrown scar.

3. _A_ Skin condition caused by pus-forming bacteria.

4. _C_ A round, firm lesion with a central crater containing keratinous material.

5. _D_ An infection with lice.

A. pyoderma
B. paronychia
C. keratoacanthoma
D. pediculosis
E. keloid

Integumentary System Disorders – Lesson 5

I. **TERMINOLOGY.**
   Enter each term in the space provided. Read the definition and description for each term.

1. **rosacea** _____

A chronic disease of the skin involving the middle third of the face and characterized by erythema, telangiectasias, papules, and pustules. This usually occurs in middle age.

2. **scabies** _____

A contagious parasitic dermatitis of both humans and animals; intense itching and secondary infection are common. This is sometimes called "The Itch."

3. **spongiosis** _____

A patchy intercellular edema of the epidermis that causes a spongy or porous appearance on microscopic examination.

4. **squamous cell carcinoma** _____

Skin cancer that arises from the malpighian cells of the epithelium. This generally occurs on sun-exposed areas but can develop anywhere. The tumor itself begins as a red papule with a scaly, crusty surface. The bulk of the tumor can actually lie below the skin, and eventually will invade underlying tissue.

5. **steatoma** _____

Fatty mass of the skin that contains follicular, keratinous, and sebaceous material. These lesions are most commonly seen on the scalp, ears, face, back, or scrotum.

6. **tinea** _____

The general term for superficial infections caused by fungi that invade dead tissues of the skin or its associated structures. This is also called "ringworm." There are different types, which are classified according to the site of involvement.

7. **tinea capitis** _____

Ringworm of the scalp. This generally affects children and is highly contagious.

8. **tinea corporis** _____

Ringworm of the body.

9. **tinea cruris** _____

Jock itch.

10. **tinea pedis** _____

Athlete's foot.

II. SPELLING.
Determine if the following words are spelled correctly. If the spelling is correct, leave the word as it has already been entered. If the spelling is incorrect, provide the correct spelling.

1. spongiosis _____✓_____   2. squamus _____SQUAMOUS_____

3. tinia _____TINEA_____   4. cruris _____✓_____

5. steatoma _____✓_____

III. TRUE/FALSE.
Mark the following true or false.

1. Scabies are not contagious.
   - ◯ true
   - ⊗ false

2. Jock itch is another name for tinea corporis.
   - ◯ true
   - ⊗ false

3. Rosacea usually occurs in middle age.
   - ⊗ true
   - ◯ false

4. A steatoma is commonly found on the scalp.
   - ⊗ true
   - ◯ false

5. Ringworm of the scalp is referred to as tinea capitis.
   - ⊗ true
   - ◯ false

Integumentary System Disorders – Lesson 6

I. TERMINOLOGY.
Enter each term in the space provided. Read the definition and description for each term.

1. **tinea unguium** _____

Ringworm of the nails.
This is also called onychomycosis.

2. **onychomycosis** _____

Ringworm of the nails.
Same as tinea unguium.

3. **toxic epidermal necrolysis** _____

A life-threatening skin disease in which the epidermis peels off in sheets.

4. **urticaria** _____

Local wheals and erythema in the dermis.

5. **vitiligo** _____

A progressive, chronic pigment anomaly of the skin manifested by white patches that may or may not be surrounded by a hyperpigmented border.

II. SPELLING.
Determine if the following words are spelled correctly. If the spelling is correct, leave the word as it has already been entered. If the spelling is incorrect, provide the correct spelling.

1. necrolisis   NECROLYSIS _____   2. unguium   ✓ _____

3. urticraia   URTICARIA _____   4. vitiligo   ✓ _____

5. onychomicosis   ONYCHOMYCOSIS _____

III. TRUE/FALSE.
Mark the following true or false.

1. Tinea unguium is also referred to as urticaria.

   ◯ true
   ⊗ false

2. Vitiligo is a progressive and chronic skin condition.

   ⊗ true
   ◯ false

3. Toxic epidermal necrolysis is life threatening.
    ⊗ true
    ◯ false

4. Urticaria involves wheals and erythema in the dermis.
    ⊗ true
    ◯ false

5. Ringworm of the nails is tinea unguium.
    ⊗ true
    ◯ false

The Eye – Introduction

As you undoubtedly know, the eye is the globe-shaped structure through which vision is accomplished. Vision is perhaps the most valued sense we as human beings have. Like other bodily organs, the eyes are protected. Photoreceptors of the eyes (which allow us to see) are protected by a bony socket. There are also protective accessory structures that help to move the eyes in their sockets. In humans, there are two eyes which are set in the front of the skull just far enough apart to achieve stereoscopic vision. It is this three-dimensional effect that enables us to assess depth. The eyes, which are obviously very important sense organs, are responsible for approximately 80% of all perceptual information assimilated.

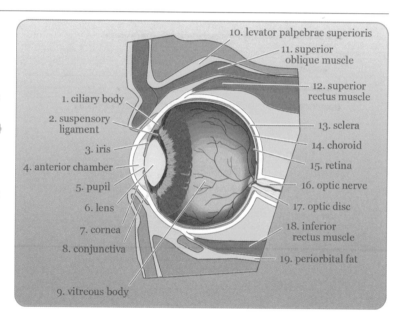

1. ciliary body
2. suspensory ligament
3. iris
4. anterior chamber
5. pupil
6. lens
7. cornea
8. conjunctiva
9. vitreous body
10. levator palpebrae superioris
11. superior oblique muscle
12. superior rectus muscle
13. sclera
14. choroid
15. retina
16. optic nerve
17. optic disc
18. inferior rectus muscle
19. periorbital fat

Term	Role in Vision Process
cornea	Captures the light rays that are reflected off the object being looked at.
lens	Brings into focus the captured light rays before they hit the retina.
retina	Sees the captured light rays as an upside down image of the object being looked at.
photoreceptors	Located in the retina, they convert the upside down image into electrical impulses.
optic nerve	Path these electrical impulses travel to reach the brain.
brain	Turns the upside down image right side up and "translates" said image into "information."

I. FILL IN THE BLANK.
Label the eye in the corresponding boxes.

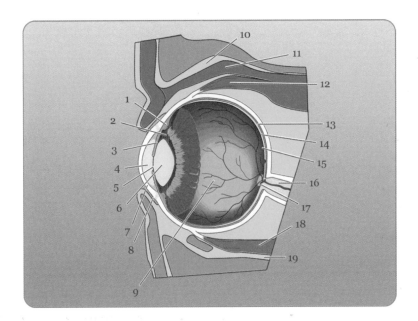

1. <u>CILIARY BODY</u>

2. <u>SUSPENSORY LIGAMENT</u>

3. <u>IRIS</u>

4. <u>ANTERIOR CHAMBER</u>

5. <u>PUPIL</u>

6. <u>LENS</u>

7. <u>CORNEA</u>

8. <u>CONJUCTIVA</u>

9. <u>VITREOUS BODY</u>

10. <u>LEVATOR PALPEBRAE SUPERIORIS</u>

11. <u>SUPERIOR OBLIQUE MUSCLE</u>

12. <u>SUPERIOR RECTUS MUSCLE</u>

13. <u>SCLERA</u>

14. <u>CHOROID</u>

15. <u>RETINA</u>

16. <u>OPTIC NERVE</u>

17. <u>OPTIC DISC</u>

18. <u>INFERIOR RECTUS MUSCLE</u>

19. <u>PERIORBITAL FAT</u>

Eye Structures

The eyeball of a human adult is approximately 1 inch in diameter. About 4/5 of the eye is positioned inside the orbit of the skull. It consists of three concentric layers, or tunics. The outermost layer, the **sclera (plural is sclerae)**, is a tough fibrous shell that forms the white of the eye. In the anterior portion the sclera changes somewhat to form the cornea, which is a convex and transparent structure. This shape allows the passage and refraction of light waves. The cornea itself consists of several layers, the innermost one being called the **Descemet** membrane, and the outermost one the **Bowman** membrane. There are no blood vessels within the sclera, although it does contain pain receptors.

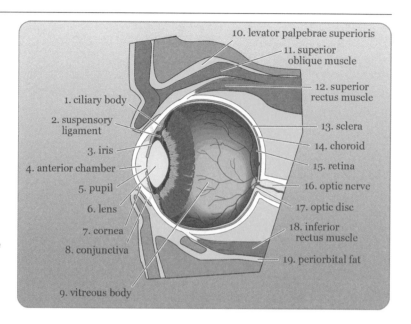

1. ciliary body
2. suspensory ligament
3. iris
4. anterior chamber
5. pupil
6. lens
7. cornea
8. conjunctiva
9. vitreous body
10. levator palpebrae superioris
11. superior oblique muscle
12. superior rectus muscle
13. sclera
14. choroid
15. retina
16. optic nerve
17. optic disc
18. inferior rectus muscle
19. periorbital fat

The second layer of the eyeball is called the choroid layer, or the **uveal tract**. It is highly vascular. The frontal portion of the choroid layer forms two separate structures: the outer ciliary body and the inner iris. The ciliary body is a muscular structure that is attached by suspensory ligaments to the lens supporting it. The ciliary body changes shape to focus. The iris is the colored portion of the eye; it is composed of smooth muscle fibers which regulate the diameter of the pupil (an opening in the center of the eye) to adjust for light. The lens is a transparent elastic structure that refracts light waves and focuses them upon the retina. The choroidal layer supplies blood to the entire eye.

The innermost layer of the eye is called the **retina (plural is retinae)**. This is a sheet of light-sensitive nerve cells containing cones and rods. Each eye has approximately 100 million rods (which respond to dim light for black-and-white vision) and 7 million cones (which percept and respond to colors in daylight). There are no cones or rods located at the point of attachment of the optic nerve. This area is technically a "blind spot" and is called the optic disc.

The eyeball itself is hollow, and the lens separates the interior into two main cavities. The iris separates the frontal portion into the anterior and posterior chambers. Both of these chambers are filled with a lymph-like fluid called the **aqueous humor**, which is secreted by the ciliary body and drains into the venous sinus. The cavity behind the lens is called the vitreous chamber and is filled with a jelly-like substance called vitreous humor.

The eyeball is protected in the head by the bones of the skull. The bone cavity holding the eyeball is lined with a layer of protective fat and is called the orbit. There are accessory organs to the eyes that also serve to protect the delicate eye structures. These are the eyebrows, eyelids (also called palpebrae), eyelashes, and the ducts that produce tears. Specifically, the eyebrows shade the eyes from the sun and prevent perspiration or other objects from getting into the eyes. Each eyelid has many lashes that protect the eye from airborne objects. The eyelids also protect the eyeball from desiccation (drying up) by reflexively blinking approximately every seven seconds. The levator palpebrae muscle raises the eyelid.

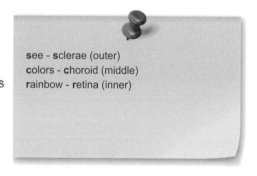

see - sclerae (outer)
colors - choroid (middle)
rainbow - retina (inner)

The eyelids also close reflexively if an object is moving towards the eye. The conjunctiva is a thin mucous membrane that lines the interior surface of the eyelid and the exposed surface of the eyeball. Tears secreted from the **lacrimal duct** constantly moisten and clean the exposed portion of the eyeball. All of these aid in the prevention of damage to the eye and preservation of vision.

The movements of the eye are controlled by the **ocular** muscles. These consist of six muscles that arise from the orbit and insert onto the outer layer of the eyeball. Four rectus muscles maneuver the eyeball in the direction indicated by their names (these are the superior, inferior, lateral, and medial rectus muscles). Two oblique muscles rotate the eyeball on its axis (these are the superior and inferior oblique muscles). The superior oblique muscle passes through a cartilage loop, much like a pulley. This loop is called the **trochlea**. All of these muscles are innervated and controlled by three cranial nerves. Both eyes move in a synchronized way due to these six muscles.

Review: Eye Structures

I. SPELLING.
   Determine if the following words are spelled correctly. If the spelling is correct, leave the word as it has already been entered. If the spelling is incorrect, provide the correct spelling.

1. siliary _CILIARY_

2. levater _LEVATOR_

3. uvial _UVEAL_

4. aqueous _✓_

5. occular _OCULAR_

6. optica _OPTIC_

7. lacrimal _✓_

8. scleraa _SCLERA_

9. conjunctivia _CONJUNCTIVA_

10. Boweman _BOWMAN_

11. iris _✓_

12. suspensatory _SUSPENSORY_

13. vitrous _VITREOUS_

14. Desquemet _DESCEMET_

15. troclea _TROCHLEA_

16. retina _✓_

17. rectis _RECTUS_

18. coroid _CHOROID_

19. paraorbital _PERIORBITAL_

20. palpebrae _✓_

II. MULTIPLE CHOICE.
Choose the term which best describes the statement.

1. Lymph-like material found in the anterior and posterior chambers.

   ⊗ aqueous humor

   ◯ aqueor humorous

   ◯ aquious humor

   ◯ aqueous humer

2. Tears are secreted from the _____.

   ⊗ lacrimal duct

   ◯ lacromal duct

   ◯ lacirimal duct

   ◯ lacrumal duct

3. The innermost membranous layer of the cornea.

   ◯ Dessemet membrane

   ⊗ Descemet membrane

   ◯ Decsemet membrane

   ◯ Descement membrane

4. The muscles of the eye are called the _____.

   ◯ occular muscles

   ◯ oculor muscles

   ◯ occuler muscles

   ⊗ ocular muscles

5. The muscle which lifts the eyelid.

   ◯ levater palpibrae superioris

   ⊗ levator palpebrae superioris

   ◯ levator palpabrae superiorus

   ◯ levator palpebrae superiorus

6. A cartilaginous loop which acts like a pulley.

   ◯ troclea

   ◯ throclea

   ⊗ trochlea

   ◯ trochlia

166

7. The innermost layer of the eye.
   - ⊙ retena
   - ⊙ retinae
   - ⊗ retina
   - ⊙ ratina

8. The ligament which supports the lens.
   - ⊗ suspensory ligament
   - ⊙ suspinsory ligament
   - ⊙ suspansory ligament
   - ⊙ suspensary ligament

9. The outermost layer of the eyeball, the shell.
   - ⊙ schlera
   - ⊗ sclera
   - ⊙ scleria
   - ⊙ scelra

10. The second layer of the eyeball.
    - ⊗ uveal tract
    - ⊙ uveal track
    - ⊙ uvial tract
    - ⊙ uveol tract

11. Another term for the second layer of the eyeball.
    - ⊙ coroid
    - ⊙ corhoid
    - ⊙ chorioid
    - ⊗ choroid

12. A muscle of the eye.
    - ⊙ superioris obliquis muscle
    - ⊙ superior obilque muscle
    - ⊗ superior oblique muscle
    - ⊙ superior obblique muscle

13. Fat around the eye structure.
    - ⊙ paraorbital fat
    - ⊙ perirbital fat
    - ⊙ perorbital fat
    - ⊗ periorbital fat

14. The aqueous humor is secreted by this structure.

   ○ siliary body
   ⊗ ciliary body
   ○ ciliiary body
   ○ celiary body

15. The outermost membrane of the cornea.

   ○ Boweman membrane
   ○ Bowmans membrane
   ⊗ Bowman membrane
   ○ Bowmon membrane

16. A jelly-like substance behind the lens.

   ○ vitreious humor
   ○ vitrious humor
   ○ vitrous humor
   ⊗ vitreous humor

17. Eyelids.

   ○ palpebra
   ⊗ palpebrae
   ○ palpibrae
   ○ palpobrae

18. The transparent structure which forms the anterior portion of the eye.

   ⊗ cornea
   ○ cornua
   ○ chornea
   ○ cornia

19. The "blind spot."

   ○ optica disca
   ○ optec disc
   ○ optiac disc
   ⊗ optic disc

20. Muscle on the top of the eye, innervated by a cranial nerve.

   ○ inferior rectus muscle
   ⊗ superior rectus muscle
   ○ superior rectis muscle
   ○ inferior rectis muscle

21. Muscle below the eye.

○ superior rectis muscle
⊗ inferior rectus muscle
○ inferior rectis muscle
○ superior rectus muscle

22. The delicate membrane which lines the eyelids and exposed portions of the sclera.

○ conjuctivia
○ conjuncitiva
○ congunctiva
⊗ conjunctiva

Disease Processes of the Eye

The eye is extremely delicate and susceptible to trauma, disease, degeneration, bacterial infection, and other problems. Think about the number of people you know personally who wear glasses—or perhaps you wear them yourself. These are necessitated by a degeneration in the visual **acuity** (clarity or sharpness) of close or distant objects, an inability to focus at any distance, spots in the visual field, or other disturbances which can be the result of various factors.

Although prolonged impairment of vision is not likely to be life-threatening, it is a terrible inconvenience and can be corrected with glasses, contact lenses, and, more recently, with laser surgery. (Surgery can permanently eliminate some kinds of visual deficiencies.) Changes in vision, brought on either suddenly or slowly over time, can indicate brain tumors or other anomalies, nerve destruction, or trauma to any of the structures associated with the eye itself.

A patient needs to be able to accurately describe visual changes to aid the health professional in the diagnosis of any disorder. The **Snellen eye chart** is the most common test given to determine visual acuity. This is the chart with the large "E" on the first line, with the letters on each line becoming progressively smaller. The patient stands 20 feet away and reads lines containing the letters of varying sizes. This is generally done with both eyes together and then alternately covering each eye. The results of this test are designated as numbers, with normal vision being 20/20. An abnormal reading, such as 20/40, indicates that the patient sees at 20 feet what an individual with normal vision sees at 40 feet.

A physician or healthcare worker also needs to inspect the eyes visually and assess reaction to light and other stimuli. A **funduscopic** examination is conducted routinely as well. This is performed using an **ophthalmoscope**, which is an instrument with a light attached and changeable lenses to account for variations in the refraction of the eye. The fundus is the back of the interior of the eye and consists of the retina, blood vessels, and optic nerve head. The funduscopic test can assist in detecting swelling or cupping of the optic disc, abnormalities associated with detachment of the retina, and vascular changes to the retina.

The use of **fluorescein dye** can aid in the detection of ulcers, foreign bodies, and injuries to the eyeball. The dye is applied to the cornea and conjunctiva, and then the surface area of the eye is examined using a **cobalt blue** light. Fluorescein can also be injected into an individual's arm and then images are taken of the retinal arteries. This process is called retinal arteriography.

An **Amsler grid** is employed to detect vision problems resulting from damage to the macula or the optic nerve. Typically the damage is caused by macular degeneration, glaucoma, or another eye disease. The grid consists of lines surrounding a central point. The patient covers one eye and focuses on the dot in the center, and notes any irregularities—wavy, blurred or distorted lines; missing or dark areas; seeing the corners and sides clearly. This is done for both eyes. **Perimetry** is a test for evaluating peripheral vision. This is accomplished by testing a patient's ability to detect flashing lights at the extreme peripheries of the visual field.

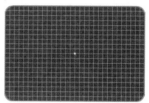

A **tonometer** is an instrument for measuring tension or pressure. Intraocular pressure, specifically of the aqueous humor, is measured on tonometry to detect the presence or absence of glaucoma.

There are other means of testing and assessing eye damage and disease. They test specific areas of visual function, such as refraction and color imaging (or conversely color blindness), x-ray or magnetic resonance imaging of the orbits, ultrasound, **gonioscopy** (to determine the angle of the anterior chamber and to demonstrate ocular motility and rotation), and injecting various agents into the eye to determine pupil response. All of these measures are employed to detect the presence or absence of various eye structure or vision abnormalities.

Review: Disease Processes of the Eye

Abnormalities of the eye are actually treated within separate specialties. Ophthalmology is the branch of medicine that deals with the eye, its anatomy, physiology, function, and pathology. Diseases of the eye, including inflammatory processes, injuries, infections, and abnormalities requiring surgical repair, are treated by an ophthalmologist in either an eye clinic, or in severe cases, within the hospital. However, problems related solely or primarily to vision are not generally treated as part of ophthalmological practice.

Optometry is the professional practice of treating vision impairment. An optometrist diagnoses, treats, and aids in the prevention of vision problems and associated disorders, as well as works to improve vision through the prescription of glasses or other functional or pharmaceutical means. Therefore, problems such as diplopia, astigmatism, amblyopia, and myopia, are in essence "treated" by an optometrist through the use of spectacles, contacts, or vision correction laser (called Lasik). If a patient requires surgical repair of traumatic or degenerative injuries, such as tears, cataracts, or diabetic retinopathies, an optometrist is not in any way responsible for treating such disorders.

Measures employed to detect the presence or absence of various eye structure or vision abnormalities are listed below and on the following page.

   I. **TERMINOLOGY.**
      Enter each term in the space provided. Read the definition and description for each term.

      1. **acuity** _____
      Sharpness of vision.

      2. **Snellen** _____
      The eye chart used to determine acuity.

3. **funduscopic** _____

Examination of the back of the retina to assess abnormalities of the optic disc.

4. **ophthalmoscope** _____

An instrument with a light attached to it for examining the eye.

5. **fluorescein dye** _____

A dye injected into the eye or the arm.

6. **cobalt blue** _____

Type of light used when examining with fluorescein dye.

7. **Amsler grid** _____

Grid used to test visual field.

8. **perimetry** _____

Testing of peripheral vision.

9. **tonometer** _____

An instrument for measuring tension or pressure.

10. **gonioscopy** _____

Examination to demonstrate ocular motility and rotation.

II. **SPELLING.**
   Determine if the following words are spelled correctly. If the spelling is correct, leave the word as it has already been entered. If the spelling is incorrect, provide the correct spelling.

1. perimetery _PERIMETRY_   2. Flouresceine _FLUORESCEIN_

3. ophthalmoscope _✓_   4. tonometer _✓_

5. Snelen _SNELLEN_   6. Amsler _✓_

7. gonoscopy _GONIOSCOPY_   8. fundiscopic _FUNDUSCOPIC_

9. accuity _ACUITY_   10. cobalt blue _✓_

III. MULTIPLE CHOICE.
Choose the term that best describes the statement.

1. Clarity or sharpness.
   - ⃝ accuracy
   - ⃝ accuity
   - ⃝ visual accuracy
   - ⊗ acuity

2. An instrument with a light attached to it, for examining the eye.
   - ⃝ funduscope
   - ⃝ gonioscope
   - ⊗ ophthalmoscope
   - ⃝ fluoroscope

3. A dye injected into the eye or the arm.
   - ⃝ cobalt blue
   - ⊗ fluorescein dye
   - ⃝ Cobalt blue
   - ⃝ fluroscope

4. A grid used in testing the visual field.
   - ⊗ Amsler grid
   - ⃝ Snellen grid
   - ⃝ tonometer
   - ⃝ Gonioscopic grid

5. An instrument for measuring tension or pressure.
   - ⃝ gonoscope
   - ⃝ fundoscope
   - ⊗ tonometer
   - ⃝ Snellen

6. Examination to demonstrate ocular motility and rotation.
   - ⃝ Snellen
   - ⃝ funduscopic examination
   - ⃝ tonometry
   - ⊗ gonioscopy

7. The eye chart used to determine acuity.

   ◯ Amsler grid
   ◯ tonometer
   ⊗ Snellen
   ◯ Gonioscopic grid

8. Testing of peripheral vision.

   ◯ peripheral acuity
   ◯ periphery
   ⊗ perimetry
   ◯ periphetry

9. Examination of the back of the retina to assess abnormalities of the optic disc.

   ◯ fluoroscopic examination
   ◯ gonioscopic examination
   ◯ perimetry
   ⊗ funduscopic examination

10. A light used on examination with fluorescein dye.

    ◯ fluoroscopic
    ⊗ cobalt blue
    ◯ fluoroscein dye
    ◯ tonometric light

Eye Symptoms and Pathologies – Lesson 1

I. TERMINOLOGY.
Enter each term in the space provided. Read the definition and description for each term.

1. **amblyopia** _____

Impairment of vision without any lesion of the eye detected.

2. **arcus senilis** _____

A white or gray band around the margin of the cornea as a result of cholesterol deposition, hyaline change, or both. This occurs with advancing age.

3. **blepharitis** _____

Inflammation of the eyelids.

4. **blepharospasm** _____

A tonic spasm of the orbicularis oculi muscle that produces more or less total closure of the eyelid.

5. **cataract** _____

An opacity on or in the lens that usually impairs vision or causes blindness. This can affect one or both eyes. There are different types of cataracts, and they are classified according to size, shape, and occurrence or by the etiology.

6. **chalazion** _____

A cystic swelling in a gland of the eyelid due to a blocked duct.

7. **chemosis** _____

Excessive edema of the conjunctiva.

8. **choroiditis** _____

Inflammation of the choroid or uveal tract.

9. **chorioretinitis** _____

Inflammation of the choroid and retina.

10. **conjunctivitis** _____

Inflammation of the conjunctiva, usually associated with a discharge.

II. SPELLING.
Determine if the following words are spelled correctly. If the spelling is correct, leave the word as it has already been entered. If the spelling is incorrect, provide the correct spelling.

1. blepharospasm _____✓_____   2. cateract _____CATARACT_____

3. chorioditis ____CHOROIDITIS____   4. conjunctivitis _____✓_____

5. arcus senilus ____ARCUS SENILIS____

III. MULTIPLE CHOICE.
Choose the best answer.

1. Inflammation of the eyelids.
   - ◯ blephariitis
   - ⊗ blepharitis
   - ◯ blepheritis
   - ◯ blephoritis

2. A band around the margin of the cornea which occurs as a result of aging.
   - ◯ arcis senilis
   - ⊗ arcus senilis
   - ◯ arcus senilus
   - ◯ arcis sanillis

3. Swelling of the eyelid due to a blocked duct.

   ○ chalazon
   ○ chalasion
   ⊗ chalazion
   ○ calasion

4. Edema of the conjunctiva.

   ○ cheimosis
   ⊗ chemosis
   ○ chiemosis
   ○ cemiosis

5. Impairment of vision without the presence of a lesion.

   ○ amblipopa
   ○ amblypopia
   ⊗ amblyopia
   ○ ambliopia

Eye Symptoms and Pathologies – Lesson 2

I. **TERMINOLOGY.**
   Enter each term in the space provided. Read the definition and description for each term.

1. **dacryocystitis** _____

Inflammation of the lacrimal sac.

2. **dacryostenosis** _____

Stricture or narrowing of a lacrimal duct.

3. **diplopia** _____

The perception of two images of a single object. Also called double vision.

4. **ectropion** _____

Eversion of eyelid edge.

5. **entropion** _____

Inversion (turning inward) of edge of lower eyelid.

6. **exophthalmos** _____

Abnormal protrusion of the eyeball (bulging eyes). This can be due either to a local process or caused by a more generalized disease, such as Graves disease. Also spelled exophthalmus.

7. **glaucoma** _____

A set of diseases in which there is increased ocular pressure caused by a failure of the aqueous humor to be absorbed. This causes changes to the optic disc and defects in the field of vision.

8. **hordeolum** _____

A localized, purulent, inflammatory bacterial infection of one or more glands of the eyelids. This is also called a stye.

9. **stye** _____

Infection of the sebaceous gland of the eyelid. Also called a hordeolum.

10. **hypermetropia** _____

Also called hyperopia, this is farsightedness. This occurs when the eyeball is too short and images are thus focused at a point behind the retina.

II. SPELLING.
Determine if the following words are spelled correctly. If the spelling is correct, leave the word as it has already been entered. If the spelling is incorrect, provide the correct spelling.

1. entropian _ENTROPION_____ 2. dacriostenosis _DACRYOSTENOSIS_

3. glaucoma _____✓_____ 4. sty _____STYE_____

5. dyplopia _DIPLOPIA_____

III. MATCHING.
Choose the correct term for the definition.

1. _A_ Inflammation of the lacrimal sac.

2. _D_ Bulging eyes.

3. _C_ Farsightedness.

4. _B_ A localized infection of a gland in the eye.

5. _E_ Eversion of the eyelid edge.

A. dacryocystitis
B. hordeolum
C. hypermetropia
D. exophthalmos
E. ectropion

Eye Symptoms and Pathologies – Lesson 3

I. TERMINOLOGY.
Enter each term in the space provided. Read the definition and description for each term.

1. **hyphema** _____

Bleeding into the anterior chamber of the eye, usually due to trauma.

2. **macular degeneration** _____

The loss of central vision due to changes in a lining of the retina. This is an age-related disorder. In this condition, peripheral vision is preserved.

3. **miosis** _____

Contraction of the pupil. This is a normal process unless related to paralysis of the dilator of the eye (paralytic miosis), caused by spasms (spastic miosis) or due to spinal disease (spinal miosis).

4. **mydriasis** _____

Physiologic or morbid dilatation of the pupil.

5. **myopia** _____

Nearsightedness. This occurs when the eyeball is elongated and light rays focus at a point in front of the retina.

6. **nystagmus** _____

An involuntary, rapid, rhythmic movement of the eyeball that can be horizontal, vertical, rotatory, or mixed. This is a symptom of systemic illness, such as multiple sclerosis or intoxication. It can also occur as a result of riding a circular ride or gazing fixedly at an object.

7. **papilledema** _____

Swelling or edema of the optic disc, usually as a result of intracranial pressure, malignant hypertension, or thrombosis of a retinal vein.

8. **photophobia** _____

Abnormal intolerance to light.

9. **presbyopia** _____

Impairment of vision due to old age. (The combining form presby- means old or denoting a relationship to old age.) This is caused by a decrease in the power of accommodation which causes the near point of distinct vision to be removed further from the eye.

10. **pterygium** _____

A thick triangular piece of tissue, pale in color, that extends medially from the nasal corneal border to the inner canthus.

II. SPELLING.
Determine if the following words are spelled correctly. If the spelling is correct, leave the word as it has already been entered. If the spelling is incorrect, provide the correct spelling.

1. myosis   *MIOSIS*
2. nystagmis   *NYSTAGMUS*
3. ptergyum   *PTERYGIUM*
4. papilledema   ✓
5. hyphema   ✓

III. MATCHING.
Match the term to the definition.

1. _E_ Nearsightedness.
2. _A_ Contraction of the pupil.
3. _H_ Involuntary rapid eyeball movement.
4. _F_ Abnormal intolerance to light.
5. _I_ Triangular piece of tissue which extends to the inner canthus.
6. _G_ Age-related disorder with central vision loss.
7. _D_ Swelling or edema of optic disc.
8. _J_ Impairment of vision due to old age.
9. _C_ Bleeding into anterior chamber of the eye.
10. _B_ Morbid dilatation of the pupil.

A. miosis
B. mydriasis
C. hyphema
D. papilledema
E. myopia
F. photophobia
G. macular degeneration
H. nystagmus
I. pterygium
J. presbyopia

Eye Symptoms and Pathologies – Lesson 4

I. TERMINOLOGY.
Enter each term in the space provided. Read the definition and description for each term.

1. **ptosis** _____
Drooping of the upper eyelid from paralysis of the third nerve or from sympathetic innervation.

2. **retinopathy** _____
A general term for degenerative, noninflammatory diseases of the retina.

3. **scleritis** _____
Inflammation of the sclera.

4. **scotoma** _____
An area of lost or depressed vision within the visual field, surrounding an area of normal vision.

5. **strabismus** _____

Deviation of the eye which the patient cannot control. This is present when the direction of gaze of the two eyes is not the same.

6. **synechia** _____

Adhesion of the iris to the cornea or the lens. (Plural is synechiae).

7. **uveitis** _____

Inflammation of all or part of the uveal tract or choroid. This condition commonly involves the other tunics as well (the sclera, cornea, and retina).

8. **xanthoma palpebrarum** _____

A soft yellow spot or plaque occurring on the eyelids, often in groups. Also called xanthelasma.

9. **xanthelasma** _____

Another name for xanthoma palpebrarum.

10. **xerophthalmia** _____

Dryness of the conjunctiva and cornea due to a vitamin A deficiency.

II. **SPELLING.**
   Determine if the following words are spelled correctly. If the spelling is correct, leave the word as it has already been entered. If the spelling is incorrect, provide the correct spelling.

1. strabysmus _STRABISMUS_   2. uveitis _____✓_____

3. scotoma _____✓_____   4. xeropthalmia _XEROPHTHALMIA_

5. synichia _SYNECHIA_

III. **MULTIPLE CHOICE.**
   Choose the best answer.

1. Inflammation of the sclera.
   - ◯ sclerytis
   - ⊗ scleritis
   - ◯ sceleritis
   - ◯ scalritis

2. Inflammation of the choroids.
   - ◯ uvitis
   - ◯ uvatis
   - ⊗ uveitis
   - ◯ uveytis

3. Dryness of conjunctiva and cornea.
   - ⊗ xerophthalmia
   - ◯ xeraphthalmia
   - ◯ xeropthalmia
   - ◯ xerapthalmia

4. Drooping of the upper eyelid.
   - ◯ tosis
   - ◯ ptysis
   - ⊗ ptosis
   - ◯ ptoses

5. A soft yellow spot occurring on the eyelids.
   - ◯ xanthema palpebrarum
   - ◯ xanthima palpebrarum
   - ◯ xanthoma palpabrarum
   - ⊗ xanthoma palpebrarum

6. Degenerative, noninflammatory disease of the retina.
   - ⊗ retinopathy
   - ◯ retanopathy
   - ◯ retenopathy
   - ◯ ritinopathy

7. Adhesion of the iris.
   - ◯ synichia
   - ◯ synachia
   - ⊗ synechia
   - ◯ synechya

8. Area of lost or depressed vision.
   - ◯ scitoma
   - ⊗ scotoma
   - ◯ scatoma
   - ◯ scetoma

9. Another name for a soft, yellow spot on the eyelids.
   - ◯ xanthilasma
   - ◯ xanthylasma
   - ⊗ xanthelasma
   - ◯ zanthelasma

10. Deviation of the eye which the patient cannot control.
    - ◯ strebisums
    - ◯ stribisimus
    - ◯ strybismus
    - ⊗ strabismus

Ear, Nose, and Throat – Introduction

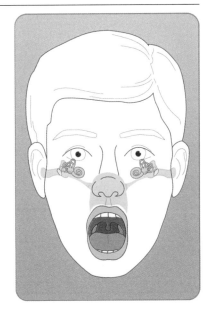

Three vital senses to the human body are hearing, smelling, and tasting. The organ responsible for both hearing and equilibrium is known as the ear. The ear is closely associated with the nose and throat, both anatomically and structurally. As a result, diseases of these structures are diagnosed and treated by a specialist called an **otorhinolaryngologist**. (This is taken from the combining forms for ear (ot(o)-), nose (rhin(o)-) and throat or larynx (laryng(o)- respectively.) All three of these structures are associated with senses, namely hearing, smell, and taste.

Smell or **olfaction** is not nearly as developed in humans as it is in other animals. We do not rely on smell to communicate or locate food sources. In fact, it is probably the least important of all the senses in terms of both maintaining proper body function and enhancing the quality of life. The olfactory sense detects the presence of odors and quickly accommodates them. Think about it. Only very strong odors maintain our attention for longer than a few minutes (skunk, sewage, burning). Other less obtrusive odors quickly leave the consciousness. However, if you leave the immediate vicinity of the odor and return to it later, you are again alert to the presence of the odor. Olfaction is very closely related to the sense of taste. In fact, if your nose is "plugged" with a cold or other disorder, you often cannot taste or even recognize foods that you usually enjoy. The olfactory, or first cranial nerve, perceives and relays information assimilated during olfaction. Some odors can also activate the fifth cranial nerve and cause reactionary responses. For example, pepper can cause sneezing, onions can make the eyes water, and ammonia (like in smelling salts) can revive an unconscious person.

The sense of taste, called **gustation**, is primarily accomplished in the mouth and especially on the tongue. The receptors which make taste possible are called taste buds. These receptors perceive four taste sensations: sweet, sour, salty, and bitter. The receptors responsible for receiving the information necessary to identify these individual taste sensations are localized on specific regions of the tongue. The structures of the tongue, soft palate, and oropharynx are part of both the digestive and respiratory systems and will be covered in subsequent sessions.

As opposed to the general senses, which are widely distributed and located throughout the body, your senses of hearing, smelling, tasting, and sight are called special senses due to their localized receptors in specific areas of the body. For example, the taste buds are the organs of taste and are located primarily on the tongue's surface. First on the plate, let's explore the ear....

Anatomy of the Ear

The most complex of the three structures treated within the medical specialty of otorhinolaryngology, both anatomically and functionally, is the ear. Although it is primarily associated with hearing, the ear actually has two important functions in the human body: it receives sound and maintains balance (equilibrium). There are specialized structures within the ear that perform these different functions. Sensations received by the ear are transmitted to the brain via the eighth cranial nerve. Anatomically, the ear is divided into three major areas: the external ear, the middle ear, and the inner ear.

The ear's three major areas are depicted in the diagram. Study this figure and move on to the associated exercises.

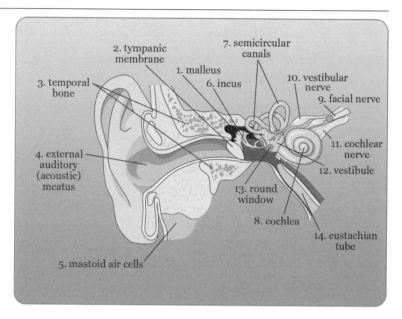

1. malleus
2. tympanic membrane
3. temporal bone
4. external auditory (acoustic) meatus
5. mastoid air cells
6. incus
7. semicircular canals
8. cochlea
9. facial nerve
10. vestibular nerve
11. cochlear nerve
12. vestibule
13. round window
14. eustachian tube

I. FILL IN THE BLANK.
Label the parts of the ear in the corresponding boxes.

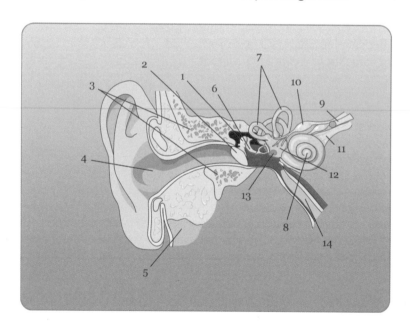

1. MALLEUS

2. TYMPANIC MEMBRANE

3. TEMPORAL BONE

4. EXTERNAL AUDITORY (ACOUSTIC) MEATUS

5. MASTOID AIR CELLS

6. INCUS

7. <u>SEMICIRCULAR CANALS</u>   8. <u>COCHLEA</u>

9. <u>FACIAL NERVE</u>   10. <u>VESTIBULAR NERVE</u>

11. <u>COCHLEAR NERVE</u>   12. <u>VESTIBULE</u>

13. <u>ROUND WINDOW</u>   14. <u>EUSTACHIAN TUBE</u>

II. FILL IN THE BLANK.
Enter each term in the space provided. Be sure to check spelling.

1. otorhinolaryngologist <u>OTORHINOLARYNGOLOGIST</u>

2. olfaction <u>OLFACTION</u>

3. gustation <u>GUSTATION</u>

The Ear and its Structures

The external ear consists of two parts: the **auricle** or **pinna**, which is the visible, fleshy appendage attached to the side of the head. This is a funnel of elastic cartilage both covered and lined by skin. The external auditory (or acoustic) meatus is a slightly S-shaped canal about 1 cm in length that extends from the outer ear into the temporal bone of the skull. The skin lining the meatus contains oil glands and specialized wax-secreting glands that produce **cerumen** (known to lay people as earwax). This acts as an insect repellent. The function of the external ear is to conduct sound waves through a gas medium to the structures of the middle ear.

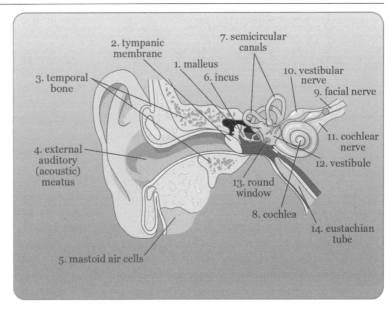

The middle ear receives the sound waves through a solid medium. The tympanic membrane receives the impulses coming in from the meatus and vibrates to set the **ossicles** in motion. The three ear ossicles are the malleus, incus, and **stapes**. These tiny bones are also called the hammer, anvil, and stirrup. They act as levers to amplify the sound received from the meatus up to twenty times. The innermost portion of the stapes attaches to the oval window in the inner ear. There are two small muscles attached to the malleus and stapes, and these contract automatically to protect the ear from loud sounds. The middle ear is connected to the nasopharynx by the eustachian tube. It is this connection that equalizes air pressure on either side of the tympanic membrane.

The inner ear, also called the **labyrinth**, contains the functional organs for hearing and equilibrium. It consists of two parts, an outer bony labyrinth that encloses an inner membranous labyrinth. The membranous labyrinth consists of tubular chambers containing fluid. A fluid also fills the space between the bony labyrinth and the membranous labyrinth. These two fluids provide a liquid medium for conduction of the vibrations involved in hearing and maintaining equilibrium. The bony portion of the inner ear is divided into three areas: the vestibule, semicircular canals, and cochlea. The vestibule is the central portion and contains the round window that the stapes fits into. The semicircular canals are primarily responsible for maintaining balance, and the cochlea is the structure involved in hearing. Receptor cells for hearing are located within the cochlear duct. A membrane extends inside the cochlear duct to form a canopy over the hair cells on the membranous floor of this duct. As the hair cells vibrate against this canopy, the mechanical forces of sound vibrations are transformed into electrical sensory impulses which are carried to the brain for interpretation.

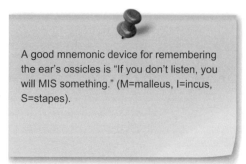

A good mnemonic device for remembering the ear's ossicles is "If you don't listen, you will MIS something." (M=malleus, I=incus, S=stapes).

The ear, much like the eye, has many built-in protective features to preserve its delicate structures and important function. The shape of the external auditory meatus and pinna not only collects sound waves, but also prevents objects and particles from entering the ear. The excretion of the ceruminous glands, muscles which autonomically contract, and position of the inner ear are also protective features. Additionally, the tympanic membrane has an unusual ability to repair itself. A ruptured "eardrum" can actually be completely healed within a single day without any outside intervention.

Review: Ear Structures

Despite the built-in preserving components of the ear, it is still susceptible to disease, trauma, degeneration, and malfunction. Before learning about specific symptomatology and disease processes, complete the following exercises that cover the structures and parts of the ear.

I. **FILL IN THE BLANK.**
   Enter each term in the space provided.

1. auricle _____   2. pinna _____

3. cerumen _____   4. ossicles _____

5. stapes _____   6. labyrinth _____

II. **SPELLING.**
   Determine if the following words are spelled correctly. If the spelling is correct, leave the word as it has already been entered. If the spelling is incorrect, provide the correct spelling.

1. incas ___INCUS___   2. cochlea ___✓___

3. olfraction ___OLFACTION___ 4. mastiod ___MASTOID___

5. labryinth ___LABYRINTH___   6. serumen ___CERUMEN___

7. gustication ___GUSTATION___   8. pinna ___✓___

9. temporol ___TEMPORAL___   10. otorhinolaryngologist ___✓___

11. vestabule ___VESTIBULE___   12. stapies ___STAPES___

13. malleolus ___MALLEUS___   14. ossicles ___✓___

15. semicirclar ___SEMICIRCULAR___   16. tympanic ___✓___

17. acustic ___ACOUSTIC___   18. oricle ___AURICLE___

III. MULTIPLE CHOICE.
Choose the term which best describes the statement.

1. The sense of taste.
   - ◯ gustration
   - ⊗ gustation
   - ◯ gastation
   - ◯ gustiation

2. The innermost ossicle of the middle ear, which attaches to the oval window in the inner ear.
   - ◯ staples
   - ◯ stapies
   - ◯ staipes
   - ⊗ stapes

3. The structure of the inner ear responsible for hearing.
   - ⊗ cochlea
   - ◯ choclea
   - ◯ chochlea
   - ◯ cochlia

4. Earwax.
   - ⊗ cerumen
   - ◯ serumen
   - ◯ carumen
   - ◯ sirumen

5. The eardrum.
   - ◯ timpanic membrane
   - ◯ tympaniac membrane
   - ⊗ tympanic membrane
   - ◯ tympanc membrane

6. One of the names given to the cartilaginous funnel attached to the side of the head.
    - ⃝ pennae
    - ⃝ pina
    - ⃝ pinia
    - ⊗ pinna

7. The ossicular hammer.
    - ⃝ maleus
    - ⃝ malleolus
    - ⃝ maleolus
    - ⊗ malleus

8. The middle ear is connected to the nasopharynx via this.
    - ⃝ ustachian tube
    - ⊗ eustachian tube
    - ⃝ eustachien tube
    - ⃝ eustashian tube

9. The inner ear.
    - ⃝ labyrinthe
    - ⃝ labrinth
    - ⃝ labryinth
    - ⊗ labyrinth

10. The ossicular anvil.
    - ⃝ incas
    - ⊗ incus
    - ⃝ inccus
    - ⃝ inchus

11. The other name given to the cartilaginous funnel attached to the side of the head.
    - ⃝ ouricle
    - ⃝ auracle
    - ⊗ auricle
    - ⃝ oracle

12. Structures responsible for equilibrium and balance.
    - ⃝ semicirclar canals
    - ⊗ semicircular canals
    - ⃝ semicercular canals
    - ⃝ hemicircular canals

13. An ear, nose, and throat practitioner.
    - ◯ othorhinolaryngologist
    - ◯ otorinolaryngolgist
    - ◯ otorinolaryngologist
    - ⊗ otorhinolaryngologist

14. Smelling.
    - ⊗ olfaction
    - ◯ olfraction
    - ◯ ollfaction
    - ◯ olfriaction

15. An S-shaped canal approximately 1 cm in length.
    - ◯ internal acoustic meatus
    - ◯ external acuostic meatus
    - ◯ external acuostic meattus
    - ⊗ external acoustic meatus

16. The structure containing the round or oval window.
    - ◯ vestabule
    - ◯ vestibuil
    - ⊗ vestibule
    - ◯ vistabule

Disease Processes of the Ear

The ear is susceptible to disease, infection, trauma, and degeneration. However, unlike other systems and organs in the body, there are relatively few symptoms associated with ear abnormalities. Hearing loss (also called deafness) is common, temporarily associated with "plugging" or other processes, but a degenerative hearing loss with age is extremely common. In fact, all of the sense organs discussed in this unit, including the skin, the eye, and the ear, degenerate significantly as we age. Environmental factors, such as prolonged exposure to loud noises, can speed up this process. A decrease in hearing or a total loss of the ability to hear anything can result. There are two primary types of hearing loss. **Conductive** hearing loss is caused by a lesion in the external auditory canal. **Sensorineural** hearing loss represents uncertainty as to whether a lesion has affected the inner ear (sensory) or the 8th nerve (neural). Sensory hearing losses are rarely due to life-threatening disorders. They are generally the result of such causes as acoustic trauma (loud noises), age, and viruses. Neural hearing losses, however, are commonly caused by tumors of the cerebellopontine angle, which are potentially fatal, or other serious neurological disorders. Hearing loss (deafness) may, of course, be partial or complete, temporary or permanent. It may be congenital or acquired in childhood, adolescence, or adulthood, and as noted, is affected by the aging process.

There are different ways that hearing can be tested, either routinely as part of a physical examination or in great detail with regard to differentiating various tones, pitches, and volumes. The first distinction that should be made in hearing loss is whether the anomaly is with air conduction or bone conduction. To test hearing by air conduction, an acoustic stimulus (a noise) is presented to the ear. This demonstrates a defect in any part of the hearing apparatus, including the external auditory canal, middle ear, inner ear, 8th cranial nerve, and the central pathways. Bone conduction is tested by placing a sound source in contact with the head; this causes vibration throughout the skull, including the walls of the cochlea and the inner ear. This method bypasses the external and middle ear and tests the viability of the inner ear, 8th cranial nerve, and central pathways.

Two types of tuning fork tests are used to differentiate a conductive hearing loss from a sensorineural hearing loss. The first, the **Weber** tuning fork test, is done by placing the stem of a vibrating tuning fork on the midline of the head and having the patient indicate in which ear he/she can hear the tone. If a conductive hearing loss is present, the individual hears the tone in the affected ear, while in a sensorineural loss it is heard in the unaffected ear. In the **Rinne** tuning fork test, the tines of a vibrating tuning fork are held first near the pinna, and then the stem of the fork (still vibrating) is placed in contact with the mastoid process. The first site tests air conduction, and the second tests bone conduction. The calculated ratio of which is heard longer and louder represents either a conductive or sensorineural hearing loss.

An **audiometer** is used to quantitate hearing loss. This is a device which transmits acoustic stimuli of specific frequencies at specific intensities using earphones to test air conduction and an oscillator to the head to test bone conduction. The actual hearing loss is then measured in **decibels**.

The **spondee threshold** is the intensity at which speech is recognized. This is tested by presenting two syllable words, accenting each syllable equally, to the patient. The ability of individuals to correctly recognize and repeat one-syllable words is called **discrimination**, and this score is reached by the percentage of words they get right upon repetition.

Tympanometry measures the effectiveness of the middle ear by placing a sound source into the external auditory canal and measuring the energy that passes through the middle ear. A tympanometer measures the movement function of the tympanic membrane.

Not all ear pathology affects the hearing. In addition to hearing loss, the major symptoms of ear pathology are vertigo, earache or **otalgia**, itching, **otorrhea** (discharge from the ear, generally purulent), and **tinnitus** (a noise in the ears, such as ringing, buzzing, or roaring which others cannot hear). **Otoscopy** is the means used to determine the underlying disease processes associated with these symptoms. An instrument that directs light into the ear and contains a magnifying lens is placed into the ear to inspect the external acoustic meatus and tympanic membrane. The mobility of the tympanic membrane can be evaluated by otoscopy during **Valsalva maneuver**. This is the forced exhalation effort against plugged nostrils and a closed mouth. The increased pressure in the eustachian tube and middle ear causes the tympanic membrane to move outward.

Neurological testing, such as finger-to-nose exercises and evaluation of gait can also demonstrate ear anomalies. CTs and x-rays of the ear structures aid in diagnosis as well.

Disease Processes of the Ear Terminology

I. TERMINOLOGY.
   Enter each term in the space provided. Read the definition and description for each term.

   1. **conductive** _____

   Hearing loss of the external canal.

   2. **sensorineural** _____

   Hearing loss of either the inner ear or cranial nerve.

   3. **Weber** _____

   A type of tuning fork.

4. **Rinne** _____

A type of tuning fork.

5. **audiometer** _____

An instrument by which the power of hearing can be gauged and recorded on a scale.

6. **decibel** _____

The unit by which sound is measured, abbreviated as dB.

7. **spondee threshold** _____

The intensity at which speech is recognized.

8. **discrimination** _____

The ability to recognize and repeat one-syllable words.

9. **tympanometry** _____

Test that measures the movement function of the tympanic membrane.

10. **otalgia** _____

An earache.

11. **otorrhea** _____

Discharge from the ear.

12. **tinnitus** _____

Ringing, buzzing, or roaring in the ears that only you can hear.

13. **otoscopy** _____

Examination of the ear using an otoscope, an instrument that directs light into the ear and contains a magnifying lens.

14. **Valsalva maneuver** _____

Plugging your nose, closing your mouth and blowing.

II. **SPELLING.**
   Determine if the following words are spelled correctly. If the spelling is correct, leave the word as it has already been entered. If the spelling is incorrect, provide the correct spelling.

1. Webber _WEBER_

2. audiometer _✓_

3. otalgea _OTALGIA_

4. conductive _✓_

5. tympanomitry _TYMPANOMETRY_

III. MULTIPLE CHOICE.
Choose the best answer.

1. The unit by which sound is measured.
   - ○ unit
   - ⊗ decibel
   - ○ milimeter
   - ○ gram

2. Discharge from the ear.
   - ○ otorhinology
   - ○ perforation
   - ⊗ otorrhea
   - ○ otosclerosis

3. The intensity at which speech is recognized.
   - ○ high threshold
   - ○ Spandee threshold
   - ⊗ spondee threshold
   - ○ sound barrier

4. The ability to recognize and repeat one-syllable words.
   - ○ threshold
   - ○ conductive hearing
   - ○ sensorineural hearing
   - ⊗ discrimination

5. Hearing loss of either the inner ear or cranial nerve.
   - ○ temporary hearing loss
   - ○ conductive hearing loss
   - ⊗ sensorineural hearing loss
   - ○ severe hearing loss

Anatomy of the Nose and Throat

In order for respiration, or breathing, to occur, the upper and lower respiratory tracts must be involved. Although the nose and throat are parts of the respiratory system, we will cover them here briefly. The nose, larynx, and pharynx are part of the upper respiratory system. The nose is composed of both bone and cartilage. The **nasal cavity** is the interior chamber of the nose; it is divided into two parts by the **nasal septum** (plural is septa). Air enters the **external nares** (nostrils, 2 in humans) and moves further along into the **internal nares** (the openings from the nasal cavity into the pharynx).

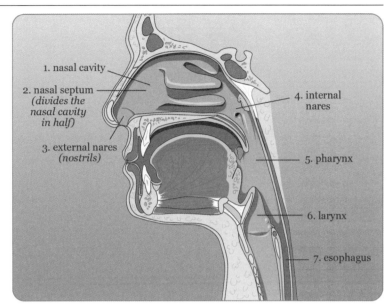

1. nasal cavity
2. nasal septum *(divides the nasal cavity in half)*
3. external nares *(nostrils)*
4. internal nares
5. pharynx
6. larynx
7. esophagus

Another name for the throat is the **pharynx**. Although covered in more detail in the respiratory systems, it is important to note that the throat is the tube that assists food in traveling from your esophagus and also carries air to the larynx and windpipe. The throat is approximately 13 cm long. The tonsils are located in the throat.

I. FILL IN THE BLANK.
Label the nose and throat in the corresponding boxes.

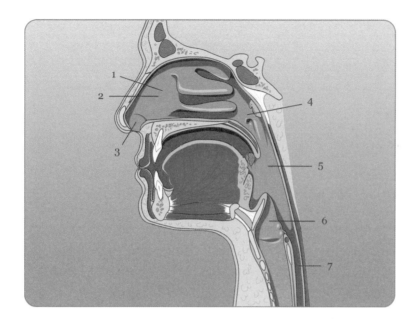

1. NASAL CAVITY

2. NASAL SEPTUM

3. EXTERNAL NARES

4. INTERNAL NARES

5. PHARYNX

6. LARYNX

7. ESOPHAGUS

II. SPELLING.
Determine if the following words are spelled correctly. If the spelling is correct, leave the word as it has already been entered. If the spelling is incorrect, provide the correct spelling.

1. pharenx   PHARYNX

2. esophagus   ✓

3. septum   ✓

4. naris   NARES

5. larnyx   ✓

Ear, Nose, and Throat Diseases – Lesson 1

Following is a list of diseases related to the ear, nose, and throat.

I. **TERMINOLOGY.**
   Enter each term in the space provided. Read the definition and description for each term.

1. **acoustic neuroma** _____

   A slowly growing, non-cancerous tumor that develops on the nerve connecting the ear to the brain.

2. **neurinoma** _____

   A tumor (usually benign) of the sheath surrounding a nerve. This is another term for a schwannoma.

3. **anosmia** _____

   Loss of the sense of smell.

4. **ceruminoma** _____

   A tumor of the ceruminous glands.

5. **cholesteatoma** _____

   A nodular growth of squamous epithelium derived from the cells in the external ear, but extending into the middle ear. This is a complication of otitis media and appears as a pearly white, shiny, formed, brittle mass.

6. **labyrinthitis** _____

   Inflammation of the labyrinth (the inner ear).

7. **mastoiditis** _____

   Inflammation of the mastoid air cells.

8. **Meniere disease** _____

   A disorder characterized by recurrent vertigo when lying down, sensory hearing loss, and tinnitus. It is associated with a dilation of the membranous labyrinth.

9. **myringitis** _____

   Inflammation of the tympanic membrane.

10. **otitis externa** _____

    Inflammation or infection of the external canal or the auricle. Swimmer's ear is one form of otitis externa.

II. MULTIPLE CHOICE.
Choose the best answer.

1. A usually benign tumor of a sheath which surrounds a nerve.
   - ◯ neuronima
   - ⊗ neurinoma
   - ◯ neurenima
   - ◯ neurenoma

2. Loss of smell.
   - ◯ annosmia
   - ◯ asnomia
   - ⊗ anosmia
   - ◯ anosmea

3. Inflammation of the tympanic membrane.
   - ◯ miringitis
   - ◯ miryngitis
   - ◯ myrengitis
   - ⊗ myringitis

4. Inflammation or infection of the external canal or the auricle.
   - ◯ otitis extrena
   - ⊗ otitis externa
   - ◯ labyrinthitis
   - ◯ labyirinthitis

5. A tumor of the ceruminous glands.
   - ◯ cerumona
   - ◯ cerumenoma
   - ◯ cerumonima
   - ⊗ ceruminoma

III. TRUE/FALSE.
Mark the following true or false.

1. A neurotome is the same as a schwannoma.
   - ◯ true
   - ⊗ false

2. A cholesteatoma appears as a pearly white mass.
   - ⊗ true
   - ◯ false

3. Mastoiditis is inflammation of the mastoid skin cells.

　○ true
　⊗ false

4. Meniere disease is characterized by recurrent vertigo.

　⊗ true
　○ false

5. Inflammation of the outer ear is referred to as labyrinthitis.

　○ true
　⊗ false

Ear, Nose, and Throat Diseases – Lesson 2

I. **TERMINOLOGY.**
   Enter each term in the space provided. Read the definition and description for each term.

1. **otitis media** _____

Inflammation of the middle ear marked by pain, fever, abnormal hearing or hearing loss, tinnitus, and vertigo. This is the most common ear infection. There are different types, such as acute otitis media, which is a bacterial infection in the middle ear, usually secondary to an upper respiratory infection; chronic otitis media, which is a permanent perforation of the tympanic membrane; and serous otitis media, which is an effusion in the middle ear which arises from incomplete resolution of an acute otitis media or obstruction of a eustachian tube.

2. **otosclerosis** _____

A condition of a bony labyrinth in which there is spongy bone formation in front of and behind the stapes, resulting in conductive hearing loss.

3. **perforation** _____

A hole made through a part or substance. A perforated tympanic membrane is a common ear problem.

4. **pharyngitis** _____

Inflammation of the pharynx (a sore throat).

5. **presbycusis** _____

The sensorineural hearing loss that occurs as a part of normal aging.

6. **rhinitis** _____

The most frequent upper respiratory tract infection; it is characterized by edema and dilation of the nasal mucous membrane, nasal discharge, and nasal obstruction.

7. **schwannoma** _____

An acoustic neurinoma; an enlarging, benign tumor usually within the internal auditory canal which arises from cells of the 8th cranial nerve.

8. **sinusitis** _____

Inflammation of the paranasal sinuses.

9. **vestibular neuronitis** _____

A benign disorder characterized by the sudden onset of severe vertigo which is persistent at first, and then becomes paroxysmal.

II. **SPELLING.**
   Determine if the following words are spelled correctly. If the spelling is correct, leave the word as it has already been entered. If the spelling is incorrect, provide the correct spelling.

   1. otitis meda _OTITIS MEDIA_   2. schwanoma _SCHWANNOMA_

   3. vestibuar neuronitis _VESTIBULAR NEURONITIS_   4. sinusitus _SINUSITIS_

   5. otosclerosis _✓_

III. **MULTIPLE CHOICE.**
   Choose the best answer.

   1. The sensorineural hearing loss which occurs as a part of normal aging.
      ⊗ presbycusis
      ○ discrimination
      ○ tinitis
      ○ rhinitis

   2. The most common ear infection.
      ○ cholesteatoma
      ○ labyrinthitis
      ⊗ otitis media
      ○ myringitis

   3. Sore throat.
      ○ otalgia
      ○ oralgia
      ○ rhinitis
      ⊗ pharyngitis

4. Nasal discharge and obstruction.
   ⊗ rhinitis
   ○ otorrhea
   ○ rhinopathy
   ○ otitis

5. Spongy bone formation behind and in front of the stapes.
   ○ schwannoma
   ○ otitis externa
   ⊗ otosclerosis
   ○ cholesteatoma

Unit 9
Brain

Brain – Introduction

The brain is one of the most complex and largest organs in the human body. The brain acts as a storage facility for so many applications, including thought, memory, consciousness, and emotion. The brain is composed of more than 10 billion neurons and weighs approximately 3 to 3 1/2 pounds. At birth, the brain is almost completely developed, with only final growth and maturation of the neurons still to occur. Upon gross examination the human brain is divided into six major regions.

The first is the **cerebrum**. This is the largest and most obvious portion of the brain. It accounts for approximately 80% of the brain's mass. It is divided into two equal hemispheres. Each hemisphere is then divided into four lobes: the frontal, parietal, temporal, and occipital (named for the cranial bones that overlie them). The lobes are divided by deep grooves called **fissures**. The surface of the cerebrum—the cerebral cortex—is deeply convoluted (like a walnut). The raised areas are called **gyri**, and the grooves in between them are called **sulci**. The cerebrum is responsible for higher mental functions including reason and memory.

While it is possible to study the anatomical features of the brain, its function is still largely a mystery to scientists. Fortunately, the field of medicine deals primarily with diagnosing, treating, and working with what is known about the brain, namely its physical makeup.

The second major structure of the brain is called the **cerebellum**. This is located below and behind the cerebrum and looks like a smaller version of it. This is responsible for coordinating muscle movement and maintaining posture.

The undersurface, or ventral portion, of the brain is made up of four major brain sections. They are, in order from the front to the back, the **diencephalon**, the midbrain or **mesencephalon**, the **pons**, and the **medulla oblongata**. The diencephalon contains some of the most vital centers of activity, including the thalamus, hypothalamus, **optic chiasm**, and pituitary gland. All impulses entering the cerebrum, except for the sense of smell, are relayed through cells in the thalamus. Specific body functions, such as hunger, thirst, sleep, body temperature, and blood pressure, are regulated by the hypothalamus. The optic chiasm is the point where the optic nerves cross. The pituitary gland is a major part of the endocrine system because of the diverse and important role it plays. The midbrain contains structures associated with visual reflexes and hearing. The pons functions as a relay center within the brain. The medulla oblongata is continuous with the spinal cord posteriorly and the pons anteriorly. It works as a relay center for the impulses to and from the spinal cord and is the nervous center that controls the heart, respiration, and vasomotor reactions. The pons and medulla oblongata together are called the brain stem.

Meninges is a term given to the three membranes that protect the brain and spinal cord. The first of these, the **dura mater**, is the outermost layer. It contacts the bones of the cranium. Underneath this is a mesh of connective tissue, thinner and more delicate than the other two layers, called the **arachnoid**. The innermost layer surrounding the surface of the brain is the **pia mater**, which is similar in makeup to the dura mater—a dense and highly vascular sheet of connective fibers.

The blood vessels of the pia mater infold and are covered by a thin layer of cells which then project into the third, fourth, and lateral ventricles of the brain. These projections are called the **choroid plexus** and are responsible for generating **cerebrospinal fluid**, which circulates through the hollow areas of the brain and spinal cord. It is then reabsorbed into the walls of the arachnoid where it drains into the circulatory system. This fluid functions primarily as a shock absorber.

Another important component of brain function is the vascular supply. In order for the brain to function at all it requires a constant and rich exchange of blood. There are two paired arteries that supply the brain with blood.

These vertebral arteries enter the cranium near the spinal cord and merge to form the basilar artery. The internal carotid arteries merge with this at the circle of Willis. Venous drainage occurs through the dural venous sinuses and then the internal jugular veins that course down the neck. All of these vessels were discussed in a previous session.

Brain Terminology

I. TERMINOLOGY.
   Enter each term in the space provided. Read the definition and description for each term.

1. **arachnoid** _____
   The thinner, more delicate middle layer of the meninges.

2. **cerebellum** _____
   The second major structure of the brain.

3. **cerebrum** _____
   Accounts for 80% of the brain's mass.

4. **choroid plexus** _____
   Projections into the brain ventricles that produce cerebrospinal fluid.

5. **commissure** _____
   A site of union of common parts.

6. **corpora quadrigemina** _____
   Part of the mesencephalon.

7. **corpus callosum** _____
   An arched mass of white matter found in the depths of the longitudinal fissure.

8. **diencephalon** _____
   Contains some of the most vital centers of body activity.

9. **dura mater** _____
   The outermost layer of the meninges that contacts the cranium.

10. **fissures** _____
    Deep grooves that divide the lobes of the cerebral hemispheres.

11. **fornix** _____
    A general term for an arch-like structure or the vault created by such a structure.

12. **genu** _____
    A general term used to describe any anatomical structure shaped like a knee.

13. **gyri** _____
    The raised portions of the cerebral surface.

14. **mammillary body** _____

Located near the pituitary gland.

15. **medulla oblongata** _____

Together with the pons, it makes up the brain stem.

16. **meninges** _____

The three membranes that protect the brain and spinal cord.

17. **mesencephalon** _____

The midbrain.

18. **neuron** _____

A general term meaning nerve cell.

19. **optic chiasm** _____

Part of the hypothalamus formed by the crossing of the optic nerves.

20. **pia mater** _____

The innermost layer of the meninges.

21. **pituitary** _____

The "master gland."

22. **septum pellucidum** _____

A triangular membrane separating the anterior horns of the lateral ventricles.

23. **splenium of corpus callosum** _____

The posterior rounded end of the corpus callosum; it conveys visual information.

24. **sulci** _____

Grooves between the gyri.

II. **SPELLING.**
   Determine if the following words are spelled correctly. If the spelling is correct, leave the word as it has already been entered. If the spelling is incorrect, provide the correct spelling.

1. cerebrum _____✓_____   2. cerebelum _____CEREBELLUM_____

3. corpis callosum _CORPUS CALLOSUM_ 4. frontle _____FRONTAL_____

5. occipital _____✓_____   6. parital _____PARIETAL_____

7. temperal _____TEMPORAL_____   8. sulcii _____SULCI_____

9. hemisphere _____✓_____   10. deincephalons _DIENCEPHALON_

III. MULTIPLE CHOICE.
Choose the best answer.

1. The raised portions of the cerebral surface.
   - ⃝ meninges
   - ⃝ sulci
   - ⊗ gyri
   - ⃝ fissures

2. A triangular membrane separating the anterior horns of the lateral ventricles.
   - ⃝ septum triangularis
   - ⃝ cortex triangularis
   - ⃝ septum oblongata
   - ⊗ septum pellucidum

3. A general term meaning nerve cell.
   - ⃝ nerve
   - ⃝ gyri
   - ⊗ neuron
   - ⃝ fornix

4. The three membranes that protect the brain and spinal cord.
   - ⃝ triplex
   - ⊗ meninges
   - ⃝ septum
   - ⃝ medulla

5. Accounts for 80% of the brain's mass.
   - ⊗ cerebrum
   - ⃝ skull
   - ⃝ cortex
   - ⃝ sulci

6. Projections into the brain ventricles that produce cerebrospinal fluid.
   - ⊗ choroid plexus
   - ⃝ fornix
   - ⃝ arachnoid
   - ⃝ medulla oblongata

7. Deep grooves which divide the lobes of the cerebral hemisphere.

○ fractures
○ gyri
○ genu
⊗ fissures

8. The posterior rounded end of the corpus callosum; it conveys visual information.

⊗ splenium of corpus callosum
○ splinium of corpus callosum
○ spalenium of corpus callosum
○ spleniem of corpus callosum

9. Together with the pons makes up the brain stem.

○ cerebrum
○ cortex
⊗ medulla oblongata
○ spinal cord

10. A general term for an arch-like structure or the vault created by such a structure.

○ crevice
○ septum
○ cortex
⊗ fornix

Midsagittal Section of The Brain

The brain is extremely intricate and complex, befitting an organ responsible for so many vital and varied processes. It will not be necessary for you to understand everything about the inner workings of the brain—after all, no one does. It is to your benefit, however, to concentrate on the spelling of these terms and know that they are located in or near the brain itself.

Below is a labeled image of a midsagittal section of the brain. Study this figure and move on to the diagram below.

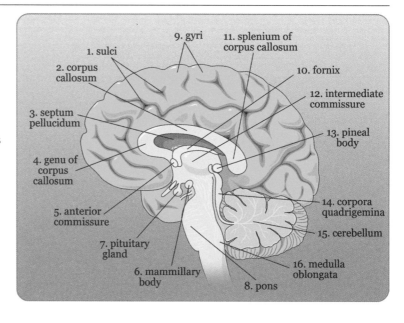

I. FILL IN THE BLANK.
Label the midsagittal section of the brain in the corresponding boxes.

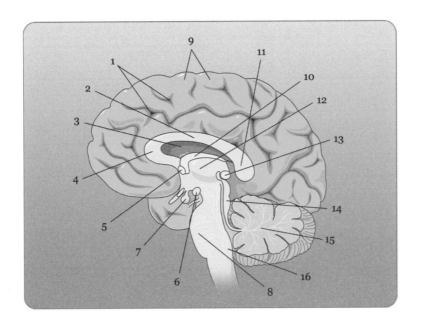

1. ___SULCI___

2. ___CORPUS CALLOSUM___

3. ___SEPTUM PELLUCIDUM___

4. ___GENU OF CORPUS CALLOSUM___

5. ___ANTERIOR COMMISSURE___

6. ___MAMMILLARY BODY___

7. ___PITUITARY GLAND___

8. ___PONS___

9. ___GYRI___

10. ___FORNIX___

11. ___SPLENIUM OF CORPUS CALLOSUM___

12. ___INTERMEDIATE COMMISSURE___

13. ___PINEAL BODY___

14. ___CORPORU QUADRIGEMINA___

15. ___CEREBELLUM___

16. ___MEDULLA OBLONGATA___

II. SPELLING.
Determine if the following words are spelled correctly. If the spelling is correct, leave the word as it has already been entered. If the spelling is incorrect, provide the correct spelling.

1. pyneal   *PINEAL*

2. pelucidum   *PELLUCIDUM*

3. sulci   ✓

4. splenium   ✓

5. comissure   *COMMISSURE*

6. mamillary   *MAMMILLARY*

7. callosum   ✓

8. neuron   ✓

9. fornix   ✓

10. cerebraspinal   *CEREBROSPINAL*

Answer Key

Disease Processes

Descriptive Terms – Lesson 1

II. SPELLING.

1. deficiency
2. degenerative
3. developmental
4. essential
5. familial
6. functional
7. hereditary

Descriptive Terms – Lesson 2

II. SPELLING.

1. idiopathic
2. infectious
3. molecular
4. neoplastic
5. nutritional
6. organic
7. traumatic

Symptomatic Terms – Lesson 1

II. MATCHING.

1. B. disease causing impairment of normal functions
2. G. persisting over a long period of time
3. H. having no symptoms
4. F. disease the patient is not born with
5. C. present at birth
6. E. progressively deteriorating condition
7. A. illness that is short and relatively severe
8. D. symptoms caused at intervals

Symptomatic Terms – Lesson 2

II. MATCHING.

1. E. abnormality continues after original disease has resolved
2. I. increasing in severity
3. D. diseases affecting newborns
4. G. disease where death is expected
5. H. disease reappears after it apparently had gone away
6. B. tends to become worse and cause death, i.e. tumor
7. C. sudden recurrence of symptoms
8. J. illness which is neither acute nor chronic
9. F. disease where most symptoms have gone away
10. A. recurrence of disease

Muscles

Anatomic and Directional Planes

II. SPELLING.

1. posterior
2. ventral
3. dorsal
4. coronal
5. medial
6. lateral
7. transverse
8. anterior
9. sagittal
10. inferior
11. distal
12. proximal

III. MULTIPLE CHOICE.

1. transverse
2. inferior
3. ventral
4. anterior
5. lateral
6. distal
7. proximal
8. medial
9. coronal
10. dorsal
11. ventral
12. posterior

Combining Planes

I. FILL IN THE BLANK.

1. ventrolateral
2. inferoposterior
3. posteroinferior
4. superolateral
5. lateroposterior
6. mediolateral
7. inferomedial
8. superoanterior
9. anteromedial
10. dorsiflexion
11. distocervical
12. anterolateral

II. SPELLING.

1. inferoposterior
2. dorsolateral
3. superoinferior
4. mediolateral
5. distobuccal
6. dorsiflexion
7. proximolateral
8. inferomedial
9. superoinferior
10. laterosuperior
11. superomedial
12. mediofrontal

III. TRUE/FALSE.

1. false
2. true
3. false
4. false
5. true
6. true
7. true
8. false

Muscles of the Face and Head

I. FILL IN THE BLANK.

1. frontalis
2. temporalis
3. orbicularis oculi
4. buccinator
5. orbicularis oris
6. triangularis
7. corrugator
8. nasalis

9. levator labii superioris
10. greater zygomatic
11. masseter
12. platysma

II. MULTIPLE CHOICE.
1. orbicularis oculi
2. triangularis
3. frontalis
4. platysma
5. buccinator
6. nasalis
7. levator labii superioris
8. orbicularis oris
9. masseter
10. greater zygomatic
11. temporalis
12. corrugator

Muscles of Facial Expression and Mastication

II. SPELLING.
1. occipitalis
2. mentalis
3. capitis
4. pterygoid
5. labii
6. risorius
7. splenius
8. inferioris

Muscles of the Neck

I. FILL IN THE BLANK.
1. trapezius
2. sternocleidomastoid
3. digastric
4. hyoglossus
5. omohyoid
6. sternohyoid

II. SPELLING.
1. omohyoid
2. trapezius
3. sternocleidomastoid
4. digastric
5. hyoglossus
6. sternohyoid

III. TRUE/FALSE.
1. false
2. false
3. true
4. false
5. true

Muscles of the Torso and Back

I. FILL IN THE BLANK.
1. trapezius
2. deltoid
3. pectoralis major
4. serratus anterior
5. linea alba
6. sternocleidomastoid
7. external oblique
8. umbilicus (belly button) OR umbilicus OR belly button
9. rectus abdominis
10. trapezius
11. deltoid
12. infraspinatus
13. teres minor
14. teres major
15. latissimus dorsi
16. gluteus medius
17. gluteus maximus
18. supraspinatus
19. rhomboid
20. erector spinae group
21. lumbar aponeurosis OR lumbar aponeurosis (previously dorsolumbar fascia)

II. SPELLING.

1. linea alba
2. umbilicus
3. pectoralis
4. serratus
5. abdominis
6. oblique
7. deltoid
8. trapezius
9. gluteus
10. rhomboid

III. MULTIPLE CHOICE.

1. rectus abdominis
2. teres major
3. lumbar aponeurosis
4. erector spinae
5. rhomboid
6. infraspinatus
7. trapezius
8. latissimus dorsi

Muscles of the Arm

I. FILL IN THE BLANK.

1. coracobrachialis
2. brachialis
3. hypothenar muscles
4. palmar aponeurosis
5. abductor pollicis brevis OR thenar muscles
6. flexor retinaculum
7. palmaris longus
8. flexor carpi radialis
9. brachioradialis
10. biceps OR biceps brachii
11. triceps
12. flexor carpi ulnaris
13. flexor digitorum superficialis

II. SPELLING.

1. coracobrachialis
2. biceps
3. ulnaris
4. brevis
5. brachialis
6. hypothenar
7. palmar
8. pollicis
9. digitorum
10. flexor
11. abductor
12. triceps

Actions of Arm Muscles

II. MULTIPLE CHOICE.

1. supinate
2. pollex
3. anconeus
4. extensor digiti minimi
5. thenar
6. brevis
7. coracobrachialis
8. retinaculum
9. biceps
10. pronator teres
11. extensor digitorum communis
12. palmaris longus
13. triceps
14. flexor digitorum profundus

Muscles of the Leg

I. FILL IN THE BLANK.

1. tensor fasciae latae
2. sartorius
3. rectus femoris
4. vastus lateralis
5. peroneus longus
6. peroneus brevis
7. lateral malleolus
8. extensor digitorum longus
9. iliopsoas
10. pectineus
11. adductor longus
12. gracilis
13. vastus medialis
14. gastrocnemius
15. anterior tibial
16. extensor hallucis longus

17. medial malleolus
18. extensor retinaculum
19. adductor magnus
20. semitendinosus
21. semimembranosus
22. soleus
23. calcaneal (Achilles) tendon OR calcaneal tendon OR Achilles tendon
24. gluteus maximus
25. greater trochanter
26. iliotibial tract
27. biceps femoris
28. peroneus longus
29. peroneus brevis

II. SPELLING.
1. malleolus
2. fasciae
3. lateralis
4. longus
5. gastrocnemius
6. hallucis
7. maximus
8. semitendinosus
9. Achilles
10. extensor

III. TRUE/FALSE.
1. false
2. true
3. false
4. true
5. false
6. false
7. true
8. false

IV. MULTIPLE CHOICE.
1. extensor retinaculum
2. iliopsoas
3. biceps
4. rectus femoris
5. semimembranosus

Review: Muscles

I. SPELLING.
1. striated
2. pterygoid
3. superficialis
4. anguli
5. latissimus
6. hallucis
7. infraspinatus
8. digitorum
9. corrugator
10. platysma

II. FILL IN THE BLANK.
1. face/head OR head OR face
2. arm
3. arm
4. arm
5. face/head OR face OR head OR neck
6. face/head OR head OR face
7. face/head OR head OR face
8. neck
9. leg
10. trunk/torso OR trunk OR torso

III. MULTIPLE CHOICE.
1. pronator teres
2. extensor digiti minimi
3. deltoid
4. lateral pterygoid
5. lateral malleolus
6. external oblique
7. greater trochanter
8. semimembranosus
9. proprioception
10. occipitalis

Disorders Affecting the Muscular System

I. TRUE/FALSE.
1. true
2. false
3. false
4. true
5. true
6. false
7. false
8. false

II. MATCHING.
1. C. a bruised or torn muscle which particularly affects the quadriceps muscle
2. E. muscle response to seizure activity
3. A. a disease caused by bacteria
4. G. wasting away or weakening of muscles
5. H. the muscular hardness of death
6. B. a chronic progressive neuromuscular weakness
7. F. a benign tumor of smooth muscle
8. D. a sac-like cavity filled with synovial fluid and located over bony prominences

III. MULTIPLE CHOICE.
1. myalgia
2. torticollis
3. Parkinson disease
4. ganglion
5. fasciculations

Arteries

Arteries of the Head, Neck, and Brain

I. FILL IN THE BLANK.
1. posterior auricular
2. external carotid
3. internal carotid
4. vertebral
5. common carotid
6. superficial temporal
7. maxillary
8. superior labial
9. inferior labial
10. facial
11. lingual
12. anterior cerebral
13. ophthalmic
14. posterior communicating
15. pontine branches
16. labyrinthine
17. superior cerebellar
18. basilar
19. anterior spinal

II. SPELLING.
1. basilar
2. cerebellar
3. ophthalmic
4. vertebral
5. cerebral
6. inferior
7. labial
8. facial
9. labyrinthine
10. auricular
11. lingual
12. carotid
13. pontine
14. branches
15. communicating

III. MULTIPLE CHOICE.
1. ophthalmic
2. vertebral
3. facial
4. pontine
5. labial
6. auricular
7. labyrinthine
8. external carotid

Arteries of the Torso – Lesson 1

II. SPELLING.
1. aorta
2. bronchial
3. innominate
4. ascending
5. subclavian

III. MULTIPLE CHOICE.
1. aorta
2. innominate
3. coronary
4. thoracic aorta
5. brachiocephalic artery

Arteries of the Torso – Lesson 2

II. SPELLING.
1. esophageal
2. cervical
3. intercostal
4. superficial
5. thoracodorsal

III. MULTIPLE CHOICE.
1. superficial
2. Cruveilhier
3. pulmonary
4. subscapular
5. phrenic

Arteries of the Torso – Lesson 3

II. SPELLING.
1. musculophrenic
2. hepatic
3. omentum
4. carotid
5. circumflex

III. MULTIPLE CHOICE.
1. splenic
2. princeps
3. gastroepiploic
4. celiac
5. pericardiophrenic

Arteries of the Torso – Lesson 4

II. SPELLING.
1. hepatic
2. cystic
3. pancreatic
4. transverse
5. suprarenal

III. MULTIPLE CHOICE.
1. circumflex
2. renal artery
3. sigmoid
4. ventral
5. mesenteric

Arteries of the Torso – Lesson 5

II. SPELLING.
1. ovarian
2. pudendal
3. abdominal
4. internal
5. external

III. MULTIPLE CHOICE.
1. ovarian
2. common iliac
3. middle sacral
4. pudendal
5. spermatic

Arteries of the Arm – Lesson 1

II. SPELLING.
1. brachial
2. collateral
3. humeral
4. axillary
5. ulnar

Arteries of the Arm – Lesson 2

II. SPELLING.
1. radial
2. carpal
3. recurrent
4. interosseous
5. dorsal

Arteries of the Arm – Lesson 3

II. SPELLING.
1. palmar
2. princeps
3. metacarpals
4. radialis
5. pollicis

Arteries of the Leg – Lesson 1

II. SPELLING.
1. femoral
2. gluteal
3. sacral
4. iliac
5. circumflex

III. MATCHING.
1. D. derived from the word 'femur,' for femur bone
2. I. supplies pelvic muscles and hip joints
3. A. near in proximity to the ilium bone
4. J. name derived from root word 'genu' meaning knee
5. E. supply blood to the gluteal region
6. H. arise from the distal aorta in the posterior pelvic area
7. F. passes out of pelvic cavity underneath inguinal ligament
8. C. supplies sacrum, coccyx, and rectum
9. G. supplies blood to external genitalia
10. B. supplies gluteal muscles and organs of the pelvis

Arteries of the Leg – Lesson 2

II. SPELLING.

1. popliteal
2. tibial
3. malleolar
4. arcuate
5. sural

III. MULTIPLE CHOICE.

1. tibial
2. arcuate
3. sural
4. popliteal
5. dorsal of foot
6. tarsal
7. peroneal
8. fibular
9. plantar
10. metatarsals

Veins

Veins – Introduction

II. MATCHING.

1. C. lymph nodes
2. A. superior vena cava
3. B. lymphatic system
4. E. inguinal
5. D. germinal centers

Veins of the Head and Neck

I. FILL IN THE BLANK.

1. temporal vein
2. occipital vein
3. external jugular vein
4. subclavian vein
5. ophthalmic vein
6. facial vein
7. superior thyroid vein
8. internal jugular vein
9. brachiocephalic vein

II. SPELLING.

1. jugular
2. ophthalmic
3. brachiocephalic
4. facial
5. occipital
6. subclavian
7. temporal
8. thyroid

III. MULTIPLE CHOICE.

1. brachiocephalic
2. ophthalmic
3. temporal
4. external jugular vein
5. occipital vein
6. facial vein
7. superior thyroid vein
8. subclavian vein

Veins of the Body – Lesson 1

II. SPELLING.
1. innominate
2. brachiocephalic
3. jugular
4. supratrochlear
5. retromandibular

III. MULTIPLE CHOICE.
1. diploic
2. internal jugular
3. supratrochlear
4. retromandibular
5. brachiocephalic

Veins of the Body – Lesson 2

II. SPELLING.
1. cephalic
2. azygos
3. antebrachial
4. plexus
5. saphenous

III. MATCHING.
1. A. hemiazygos
2. D. plexus
3. E. cephalic
4. C. saphenous
5. B. basilic

Bones

Bones and Joints

I. FILL IN THE BLANK.
1. epiphysis
2. metaphysis
3. diaphysis
4. periosteum
5. endosteum

II. SPELLING.
1. epiphysis
2. cortical
3. periosteum
4. lacunae
5. canaliculi
6. metaphysis
7. osteocytes
8. endosteum
9. diaphysis
10. cancellous

III. MULTIPLE CHOICE.
1. Lacunae
2. cancellous
3. diaphysis
4. Endosteum
5. cortical
6. metaphysis
7. Canaliculi
8. Epiphysis
9. periosteum
10. Osteocytes

Axial Skeleton – Skull (Part B)

I. FILL IN THE BLANK.

1. coronal suture
2. sphenoid bone
3. nasal bone
4. frontal bone
5. temporal bone
6. nasal concha
7. maxilla
8. parietal bone
9. squamous suture
10. lambdoid suture
11. occipital bone
12. mastoid process
13. styloid process
14. condyloid process
15. coronoid process
16. supraorbital foramen
17. lacrimal bone
18. zygomatic bone
19. vomer
20. mandible

II. SPELLING.

1. ethmoid
2. coronal
3. sphenoid
4. concha
5. vomer
6. mandible
7. foramen
8. supraorbital
9. occipital
10. squamous
11. nasal
12. maxilla
13. lacrimal
14. zygomatic
15. parietal
16. temporal
17. condyloid
18. frontal
19. lambdoid
20. coronoid

III. MULTIPLE CHOICE.

1. ethmoid
2. occipital
3. nasal
4. Concha
5. mandible
6. Zygomatic
7. foramen
8. maxilla
9. lambdoid
10. Condyloid

Axial Skeleton – Vertebral Column

I. FILL IN THE BLANK.

1. atlas
2. axis
3. cervical spine
4. thoracic spine
5. lumbar spine
6. sacral spine
7. coccygeal OR coccyx OR coccygeal (coccyx)
8. lumbosacral joint

II. MATCHING.

1. G. lower back
2. F. between the bones of the spine
3. B. the neck
4. E. connects to the ribs
5. D. join
6. A. triangular shaped
7. C. tailbone

III. FILL IN THE BLANK.

1. lumbar spine
2. Articulate
3. cervical spine
4. sacral spine
5. thoracic spine
6. coccyx
7. intervertebral discs

Appendicular Skeleton

I. FILL IN THE BLANK.

1. vertebrae
2. sternum
3. ribs
4. ilium
5. sacrum
6. pubis
7. coccyx
8. ischium
9. femur
10. patella
11. tibia
12. fibula
13. tarsals
14. metatarsals
15. phalanges
16. cranium OR skull OR cranium/skull
17. clavicle
18. scapula
19. humerus
20. ulna
21. radius
22. carpals
23. metacarpals
24. phalanges

II. FILL IN THE BLANK.

1. sternum
2. ilium OR sacrum OR coccyx
3. sacrum OR ilium OR coccyx
4. coccyx OR ilium OR sacrum
5. tarsals OR metatarsals OR phalanges
6. metatarsals OR phalanges OR tarsals
7. phalanges OR tarsals OR metatarsals
8. fibula OR patella
9. patella OR fibula
10. clavicle OR scapula
11. scapula OR clavicle
12. vertebrae
13. ribs
14. humerus OR ulna
15. ulna OR humerus
16. cranium OR skull
17. skull OR cranium
18. carpals OR metacarpals OR phalanges
19. metacarpals OR carpals OR phalanges
20. phalanges OR metacarpals OR carpals

Appendicular Skeleton – Diagram

I. SPELLING.

1. pubis
2. radius
3. carpals
4. patella
5. ischium
6. ilium
7. coccyx
8. tarsals
9. vertebrae
10. clavicle

Appendicular Skeleton – Shoulder Bones

I. TRUE/FALSE.

1. false
2. true
3. true
4. false
5. false

II. MULTIPLE CHOICE.

1. long bone
2. S
3. humerus
4. epicondyle
5. scapula

Appendicular Skeleton – Arm Bones

II. MATCHING.
1. G. fingers
2. C. pinky-side bone
3. D. wrists
4. H. prominence
5. A. hands
6. E. point of elbow
7. F. joint of the ulna and radius
8. B. thumb-side bone

III. MULTIPLE CHOICE.
1. ulna
2. radius
3. malleolus
4. tuberosity
5. styloid process

Appendicular Skeleton – Hip and Upper Leg

I. MATCHING.
1. B. thigh bone
2. D. lower part of the "eye mask"
3. C. the head of the femur fits into this
4. E. hip bone
5. A. kneecap

II. MULTIPLE CHOICE.
1. ischium
2. trochanter
3. acetabulum
4. medial and lateral epicondyles
5. femur

Appendicular Skeleton – Lower Leg and Foot

I. MATCHING.
1. B. feet bones
2. A. ankle bone(s)
3. D. toes
4. E. protects the ankle
5. C. larger lower leg bone

II. MULTIPLE CHOICE.
1. 14
2. fibula
3. tibia
4. epicondyle
5. arches

Review: Lower Appendicular Bones

II. TRUE/FALSE.
1. false
2. false
3. true
4. false
5. false

III. TRUE/FALSE.
1. false
2. true
3. false
4. false
5. true

Types of Bones

II. FILL IN THE BLANK.

1. sesamoid
2. flat
3. short
4. long
5. wormian
6. flat
7. long
8. short
9. irregular
10. irregular

Joint Names

II. SPELLING.

1. costovertebral
2. humeroulnar
3. manubriosternal
4. iliosacral
5. carpometacarpal
6. cricoarytenoid
7. radioulnar
8. cricothyroid
9. incudostapedial
10. glenohumeral

III. TRUE/FALSE.

1. false
2. true
3. false
4. true
5. true
6. false
7. false
8. true
9. true
10. false

Joint Movement – Lesson 1

II. MATCHING.

1. E. unbending
2. B. bending
3. C. moving away from midline
4. D. adding a part back to the body
5. A. circling

III. FILL IN THE BLANK.

1. flexion
2. extension
3. circumduction
4. Extension
5. Flexion

Joint Movement – Lesson 2

II. MATCHING.

1. D. flexing the foot
2. C. pointing the toe
3. E. around an axis
4. B. lying face up
5. A. lying face down

III. FILL IN THE BLANK.

1. prone
2. Rotation
3. plantar flexion
4. dorsiflexion
5. supine

IV. MULTIPLE CHOICE.

1. movement of the foot that brings the top of the foot closer to the leg
2. move with ease
3. flexion
4. movement in a circle
5. prone
6. joint
7. fibrous, cartilaginous, synovial
8. synovial joints
9. multiaxial
10. somewhat moveable

Bone/Muscle Attachment

II. TRUE/FALSE.

1. false
2. true
3. true
4. false
5. false

Ligaments

II. MATCHING.

1. A. shaped like a cross
2. E. yellow ligament
3. B. support
4. D. like a raven's beak
5. C. indirect

III. FILL IN THE BLANK.

1. coracoid
2. accessory
3. cruciate
4. arcuate
5. collateral

Sensory Organs

Skin Structures – Lesson 1

II. FILL IN THE BLANK.

1. epidermis
2. papillary layer
3. reticular layer
4. dermis
5. subcutaneous layer
6. sebaceous gland
7. arrector pili muscle
8. sudoriferous gland
9. pacinian corpuscle

Review: Skin Structures

I. SPELLING.

1. reticular
2. dermis
3. desiccation
4. arrector
5. squamous
6. subcuticular
7. subcutaneous
8. eponychium
9. sudoriferous
10. epithelium
11. epidermis
12. papillary
13. keratin
14. stratified
15. sebaceous
16. corpuscle

II. MULTIPLE CHOICE.

1. eponychium
2. keratin
3. dermis
4. sebaceous
5. subcuticular
6. desiccation
7. papillary
8. stratified squamous epithelium
9. subcutaneous layer
10. arrector pili
11. reticular
12. sudoriferous gland
13. pacinian corpuscle
14. epidermis

Skin Abnormalities – Lesson 1

II. SPELLING.

1. bleb
2. abrasion
3. comedo
4. bulla
5. cicatrix

III. MULTIPLE CHOICE.

1. callus
2. comedo
3. contusion
4. bulla
5. cicatrix

Skin Abnormalities – Lesson 2

II. SPELLING.

1. lichenification
2. papule
3. eschar
4. ecchymosis
5. nevus

III. MULTIPLE CHOICE.

1. ecchymosis
2. papule
3. eschar
4. furuncle
5. nevus

Skin Abnormalities – Lesson 3

II. SPELLING.

1. verrucae
2. pruritus
3. purpura
4. wheal
5. petechia
6. psoriatic

III. MULTIPLE CHOICE.

1. telangiectasia
2. wheal
3. verrucae
4. pruritus
5. petechia

Integumentary System Disorders – Lesson 1

II. SPELLING.

1. acne
2. actinic keratosis OR keratosis
3. basal cell carcinoma OR basal
4. burn
5. dandruff

III. MULTIPLE CHOICE.

1. alopecia
3. abscess
5. decubitus ulcer

2. candidiasis
4. cellulitis

Integumentary System Disorders – Lesson 2

II. SPELLING.

1. stasis
3. eczema
5. erythema

2. dermatitis
4. nummular

III. TRUE/FALSE.

1. false
3. true
5. false

2. false
4. true

Integumentary System Disorders – Lesson 3

II. SPELLING.

1. nodosum
3. hemangioma
5. impetigo

2. putrefaction
4. hidradenitis suppurativa OR suppurativa

III. FILL IN THE BLANK.

1. gangrene
3. folliculitis
5. ichthyosis

2. hemangioma
4. erythema multiforme

Integumentary System Disorders – Lesson 4

II. SPELLING.

1. Kaposi sarcoma OR Kaposi
3. melanoma
5. psoriasis

2. mycosis fungoides
4. pityriasis rosea OR rosea

III. MATCHING.

1. B. paronychia
3. A. pyoderma
5. D. pediculosis

2. E. keloid
4. C. keratoacanthoma

Integumentary System Disorders – Lesson 5

II. SPELLING.

1. spongiosis
3. tinea
5. steatoma

2. squamous
4. cruris

III. TRUE/FALSE.

1. false
3. true
5. true

2. false
4. true

Integumentary System Disorders – Lesson 6

II. SPELLING.
1. necrolysis
2. unguium
3. urticaria
4. vitiligo
5. onychomycosis

III. TRUE/FALSE.
1. false
2. true
3. true
4. true
5. true

The Eye – Introduction

I. FILL IN THE BLANK.
1. ciliary body
2. suspensory ligament
3. iris
4. anterior chamber
5. pupil
6. lens
7. cornea
8. conjunctiva
9. vitreous body
10. levator palpebrae superioris
11. superior oblique muscle
12. superior rectus muscle
13. sclera
14. choroid
15. retina
16. optic nerve
17. optic disc
18. inferior rectus muscle
19. periorbital fat

Review: Eye Structures

I. SPELLING.
1. ciliary
2. levator
3. uveal
4. aqueous
5. ocular
6. optic
7. lacrimal
8. sclera OR sclerae
9. conjunctiva
10. Bowman
11. iris
12. suspensory
13. vitreous
14. Descemet
15. trochlea
16. retina
17. rectus
18. choroid
19. periorbital
20. palpebrae

II. MULTIPLE CHOICE.
1. aqueous humor
2. lacrimal duct
3. Descemet membrane
4. ocular muscles
5. levator palpebrae superioris
6. trochlea
7. retina
8. suspensory ligament
9. sclera
10. uveal tract
11. choroid
12. superior oblique muscle
13. periorbital fat
14. ciliary body
15. Bowman membrane
16. vitreous humor
17. palpebrae
18. cornea
19. optic disc
20. superior rectus muscle
21. inferior rectus muscle
22. conjunctiva

Review: Disease Processes of the Eye

II. SPELLING.

1. perimetry
2. fluorescein
3. ophthalmoscope
4. tonometer
5. Snellen
6. Amsler
7. gonioscopy
8. funduscopic
9. acuity
10. cobalt blue

III. MULTIPLE CHOICE.

1. acuity
2. ophthalmoscope
3. fluorescein dye
4. Amsler grid
5. tonometer
6. gonioscopy
7. Snellen
8. perimetry
9. funduscopic examination
10. cobalt blue

Eye Symptoms and Pathologies – Lesson 1

II. SPELLING.

1. blepharospasm
2. cataract
3. choroiditis
4. conjunctivitis
5. arcus senilis OR senilis

III. MULTIPLE CHOICE.

1. blepharitis
2. arcus senilis
3. chalazion
4. chemosis
5. amblyopia

Eye Symptoms and Pathologies – Lesson 2

II. SPELLING.

1. entropion
2. dacryostenosis
3. glaucoma
4. stye
5. diplopia

III. MATCHING.

1. A. dacryocystitis
2. D. exophthalmos
3. C. hypermetropia
4. B. hordeolum
5. E. ectropion

Eye Symptoms and Pathologies – Lesson 3

II. SPELLING.

1. miosis
2. nystagmus
3. pterygium
4. papilledema
5. hyphema

III. MATCHING.

1. E. myopia
2. A. miosis
3. H. nystagmus
4. F. photophobia
5. I. pterygium
6. G. macular degeneration
7. D. papilledema
8. J. presbyopia
9. C. hyphema
10. B. mydriasis

II. SPELLING.

1. strabismus
2. uveitis
3. scotoma
4. xerophthalmia
5. synechia

III. MULTIPLE CHOICE.

1. scleritis
2. uveitis
3. xerophthalmia
4. ptosis
5. xanthoma palpebrarum
6. retinopathy
7. synechia
8. scotoma
9. xanthelasma
10. strabismus

Anatomy of the Ear

I. FILL IN THE BLANK.

1. malleus
2. tympanic membrane
3. temporal bone
4. external acoustic meatus OR external auditory meatus OR external auditory (acoustic) meatus
5. mastoid air cells
6. incus
7. semicircular canals
8. cochlea
9. facial nerve
10. vestibular nerve
11. cochlear nerve
12. vestibule
13. round window
14. eustachian tube

Review: Ear Structures

II. SPELLING.

1. incus
2. cochlea
3. olfaction
4. mastoid
5. labyrinth
6. cerumen
7. gustation
8. pinna
9. temporal
10. otorhinolaryngologist
11. vestibule
12. stapes
13. malleus
14. ossicles
15. semicircular
16. tympanic
17. acoustic
18. auricle

III. MULTIPLE CHOICE.

1. gustation
2. stapes
3. cochlea
4. cerumen
5. tympanic membrane
6. pinna
7. malleus
8. eustachian tube
9. labyrinth
10. incus
11. auricle
12. semicircular canals
13. otorhinolaryngologist
14. olfaction
15. external acoustic meatus
16. vestibule

Disease Processes of the Ear Terminology

II. SPELLING.
1. Weber
2. audiometer
3. otalgia
4. conductive
5. tympanometry

III. MULTIPLE CHOICE.
1. decibel
2. otorrhea
3. spondee threshold
4. discrimination
5. sensorineural hearing loss

Anatomy of the Nose and Throat

I. FILL IN THE BLANK.
1. nasal cavity
2. nasal septum
3. external nares
4. internal nares
5. pharynx
6. larynx
7. esophagus

II. SPELLING.
1. pharynx
2. esophagus
3. septum
4. nares
5. larynx

Ear, Nose, and Throat Diseases – Lesson 1

II. MULTIPLE CHOICE.
1. neurinoma
2. anosmia
3. myringitis
4. otitis externa
5. ceruminoma

III. TRUE/FALSE.
1. false
2. true
3. false
4. true
5. false

Ear, Nose, and Throat Diseases – Lesson 2

II. SPELLING.
1. otitis media OR media
2. schwannoma
3. vestibular neuronitis
4. sinusitis
5. otosclerosis

III. MULTIPLE CHOICE.
1. presbycusis
2. otitis media
3. pharyngitis
4. rhinitis
5. otosclerosis

Brain Terminology

II. SPELLING.

1. cerebrum
2. cerebellum
3. corpus callosum OR corpus
4. frontal
5. occipital
6. parietal
7. temporal
8. sulci
9. hemisphere
10. diencephalon OR diencephalons

III. MULTIPLE CHOICE.

1. gyri
2. septum pellucidum
3. neuron
4. meninges
5. cerebrum
6. choroid plexus
7. fissures
8. splenium of corpus callosum
9. medulla oblongata
10. fornix

Midsagittal Section of The Brain

I. FILL IN THE BLANK.

1. sulci
2. corpus callosum
3. septum pellucidum
4. genu of corpus callosum
5. anterior commissure
6. mammillary body
7. pituitary gland
8. pons
9. gyri
10. fornix
11. splenium of corpus callosum
12. intermediate commissure
13. pineal body
14. corpora quadrigemina
15. cerebellum
16. medulla oblongata

II. SPELLING.

1. pineal
2. pellucidum
3. sulci
4. splenium
5. commissure
6. mammillary
7. callosum
8. neuron
9. fornix
10. cerebrospinal